PRAISE FOR *COLLABORATIVE PROFESSIONALISM*

Accessible and deep in equal measure, *Collaborative Professionalism* gives us vivid, creative designs for engaging in lasting collaboration. This is a book that will have the ear of teachers, teachers' leaders, and policy makers all over the world.

Michael Fullan, Professor Emeritus
OISE/University of Toronto

In many countries, the preferred political strategy to raise standards in education is relentless competition: between students, teachers, schools, and districts. On the whole, it isn't working. There is a better way: collaboration. Human beings are intensely social creatures and much of what we can and do achieve comes from our capacity for working together. In this illuminating and highly practical book, the authors show why and how collaboration is the real driver of educational transformation, for our students, teachers, and schools.

Sir Ken Robinson, Educator and
New York Times Best-Selling
Author of You, Your Child, and School

Collaborative Professionalism makes an impressive contribution to the development of teaching and improving schools by stressing the importance of investing in social capital. Building on their rich experiences and vivid case studies from around the world, the authors promote collaborative professionalism as the next big step in the global movement for educational improvement. This brilliantly written book is a must-read for teachers, leaders, policy makers, and those who wish to become collaborative professionals.

ki Institute for Education,
UNSW Sydney, Australia

I strongly recommend *Collaborative Professionalism* to education policy makers, school leaders, and teacher activists. It inspires reflection on strengthening the teaching profession, at a time of unprecedented threat from technology, retention, and narrow accountability. The book combines a readable style with tangible case studies and clear recommendations on what should be done now to foster a healthy future for the most important of professions—working in alliance, with trusted autonomy, and an agility to deal with a time of unprecedented change.

Lord Jim Knight, former Schools Minister
and Chief Education Officer,
Times Education Supplement, UK

This wonderful book starts with the proposition that our central question is not whether educators can make a significant difference in the well-being and capabilities of the children we serve and the communities in which they live, but whether we are willing to do so. Our work as educators is urgent; every minute matters for our most school-dependent children. This book is a powerful reminder that getting better is something we do together.

Rebecca Holcombe, former Secretary
of Education for Vermont

Hargreaves and O'Connor have written an extraordinary book explaining, deepening, and teaching us how to transform teaching and learning in schools. We learn how people collaborate in five different contexts and cultures across the globe. And we finally understand the important stages of building positive, trusting, thoughtful, and lasting collaborative professionalism with all its significant details.

Ann Lieberman, Senior Scholar at Stanford University

Collaborative Professionalism

Corwin Impact Leadership Series

Series Editor: Peter M. DeWitt

Collaborative Professionalism

When Teaching Together Means Learning for All

Andy Hargreaves

Michael T. O'Connor

Corwin Impact Leadership Series

Series Editor: Peter M. DeWitt

A SAGE Publishing Company

world innovation summit for education

مؤتمر القمة العالمي للابتكار في التعليم

an initiative of مؤسسة قطر Qatar Foundation

FOR INFORMATION:

Corwin

A SAGE Company

2455 Teller Road

Thousand Oaks, California 91320

(800) 233-9936

www.corwin.com

SAGE Publications Ltd.

1 Oliver's Yard

55 City Road

London EC1Y 1SP

United Kingdom

SAGE Publications India Pvt. Ltd.

B 1/I 1 Mohan Cooperative Industrial Area

Mathura Road, New Delhi 110 044

India

SAGE Publications Asia-Pacific Pte. Ltd.

3 Church Street

#10-04 Samsung Hub

Singapore 049483

Publisher: Arnis Burvikovs

Development Editor: Desireé A. Bartlett

Editorial Assistant: Eliza Erickson

Production Editor: Andrew Olson

Copy Editor: Erin Livingston

Typesetter: C&M Digitals (P) Ltd.

Proofreader: Sarah J. Duffy

Indexer: Scott Smiley

Cover Designer: Michael Dubowe

Marketing Manager: Nicole Franks

Printed in the United States of America

Names: Hargreaves, Andy, author. | O'Connor, Michael T. (Michael Thomas), author.

Title: Collaborative professionalism : when teaching together means learning for all / Andy Hargreaves, Michael T. O'Connor.

Description: First edition. | Thousand Oaks, California : Corwin, a SAGE Company, [2018] | Series: Corwin impact leadership series | Includes bibliographical references and index.

Identifiers: LCCN 2018006076| ISBN 9781506328157 (paperback ; alkaline paper) | ISBN 1506328156 (paperback ; alkaline paper)

Subjects: LCSH: Teachers—In-service training—Cross-cultural studies. | Teachers—Professional relationships—Cross-cultural studies. | Professional learning communities—Cross-cultural studies.

Classification: LCC LB1731 .H2675 2018 | DDC 370.71/1—dc23 LC record available at https://lccn.loc.gov/2018006076

This book is printed on acid-free paper.

SUSTAINABLE FORESTRY INITIATIVE

Certified Chain of Custody
At Least 10% Certified Forest Content
www.sfiprogram.org
SFI-01028

19 20 21 22 10 9 8 7 6 5 4 3

Contents

List of Abbreviations and Acronyms

CBC	Canadian Broadcasting Corporation
CI	collaborative inquiry
CMO	Charter Management Organization
ELA	English Language Arts
EQAO	Education Quality and Accountability Office of Ontario
FNMI	First Nations, Métis, and Inuit
NW RISE	Northwest Rural Innovation and Student Engagement
OECD	Organisation for Economic Co-operation and Development
PACT	Providence Alliance for Catholic Teachers
PD	professional development
PISA	Program for International Student Assessment
PLC	professional learning community
SEA	state education agency
SRL	self-regulated learning

TIMMS   Third International Maths and Science Studies

TNTP   The New Teacher Project

UNESCO   United Nations Educational, Scientific
           and Cultural Organization

Preface

This book is about how teachers and other educators can and do collaborate. With different colleagues, I've been studying and supporting collaboration among educators for 30 years. We've looked at whether and why elementary teachers use their time outside the classroom in individual or collaborative ways. We've analyzed how high school teachers tend to collaborate in separate subgroups, often defined by their subject departments. We've investigated what factors create positive and negative emotions in teachers' relationships with their colleagues. We've studied and supported the design and development of teacher networks in Canada, the United Kingdom, and the United States. We've examined how school districts can assist each other in their mutual improvement efforts. We've even set up a collaborative of education ministers and professional leaders in nine countries to serve as critical friends for each other as they strive to create greater equity and inclusion for all their students.

So, I know a lot about collaboration among educators and about how to build it in practice. At least, this is what I thought when an opportunity arose with the WISE Foundation to conduct a 1-year research project in relation to some aspect of educational change. Since I knew so much, I thought that my colleague Michael O'Connor and I could simply take some of the frameworks we had already developed and illustrate them practically with a set of international case studies. We could take our existing knowledge and apply it to a range of varying systems.

Were we ever wrong! For example, we discovered how collaboration can vary a lot, depending on what country or culture you are in. I should have known this after my experience of moving from

England to Canada in 1987. As a young scholar in England at the time, I had been used to more senior colleagues telling me my ideas wouldn't work or get funded. I lived my professional life feeling as if I had to argue and advocate for everything to have a chance of getting anything accepted at all. Once I'd arrived in Canada, however, colleagues in the university and school systems responded to ideas and suggestions by asking me how they could support them. They invited me into networks, partnerships, and other kinds of collaboration. Most of my ideas (which were now *our* ideas) got accepted and, all of a sudden, I found I had a whole lot more work to do!

After about a year or so, it occurred to me that something about me had changed. In England, when I was teaching or lecturing, my body language had been animated, but rather sharp and choppy—a bit like former Prime Minister Tony Blair. In Canada, though, my body language was changing and, without really thinking about it, I was now starting to make more rounded, inviting movements with my hands. In a good way, collaboration can really get under the skin—and just how it does this shifts from one culture to another. These are things to bear in mind when we consider how to take an interesting design for teacher collaboration—such as lesson study in Asia or professional learning communities (PLCs) in the United States—and adapt it to a different culture somewhere else.

Something else we have learned by studying different examples of collaboration is how the ways that people collaborate are also changing over time. They are becoming more precise in their methods, more embedded in deeper professional relationships, and more widespread throughout everyday practice. At its best, collaboration is becoming more formal and more informal, more precise and more pervasive. Through the examples we have studied and the literature we have consulted, we believe there have been five evolutionary stages of professional collaboration. After a long period in which the culture of teaching was one of individualism and where professional collaboration was largely absent, there have been four succeeding stages:

1. *Emergence*: Professional collaboration is an alternative to individualism. Research demonstrates the positive impact of professional collaboration on student learning and achievement.

2. *Doubt*: Some forms of professional collaboration are found to be too weak in their overreliance on talk rather than action. Others (known as *contrived collegiality*) are too forced when they are used to implement top-down mandates.

3. *Design*: Specific models of professional collaboration are created in the form of PLCs, data teams, collaborative action research, and so on.

4. *Transformation*: Professional collaboration transitions to deeper forms of *collaborative professionalism* that are more precise in their structures and methods, more pervasive in their presence, throughout all aspects of teachers' practice rather than taking the shape of add-on meetings, and more rooted in positive and trusting relationships among the people involved.

One key feature of effective collaboration is a peculiar combination of pride and humility. Pride is about acknowledging one's own expertise and not being reticent about admitting it and offering it. Holding back on one's own expertise for reasons of politeness or due to hesitancy about causing offense by appearing to be boastful or narcissistic is false humility—it withholds precious knowledge and insight from colleagues and all the children they serve.

Genuine humility is about recognizing that while we have important things to contribute as professionals, none of us knows everything. Genuine humility enables colleagues to pool all their ideas and insights, their own bits of imperfect and incomplete knowledge, to try to solve the mysteries of how to help the child learn and develop. It enables leaders to share and distribute their leadership, to release the knowledge and expertise possessed by others. Admitting that, at first, we often don't really know what the issue might be is part of our professionalism. Inquiring together and acting upon it is the essence of *collaborative* professionalism.

We would be wrong to say we didn't know much about professional collaboration before we started this project and wrote this report. We knew a great deal about collaboration from three decades of doing it and studying it. But we didn't know everything, and after a while, we realized we knew a lot less than we thought we did.

We have learned to appreciate how many aspects of collaboration vary across cultures and systems. We have learned that it is growing and progressing in many places to deeper forms of what we call collaborative professionalism. We have learned a lot from each other as fellow researchers and also appreciate how much we owe to all those in the field, starting with Willard Waller in his book *The Sociology of Teaching* in 1932, whose worked blazed many trails in this terrain before ours.

We have also really benefitted from not only studying what teachers say about how they collaborate but also watching and listening to how they collaborate in practice—from the mountains of Colombia to the tower blocks of Hong Kong and the remote communities of Canada and the U.S. Pacific Northwest. We have had to learn how to write about this work differently from our usual scholarly style—to become magazine writers as much as university researchers, to treat our writing not only as a form of accurate reporting but also as an act of engagement through teaching. We have written badly before we have written better. We are still trying to help each other improve, as we know you are, too. Collaboration can make us better as writers, teachers, researchers, and all kinds of fellow professionals. But not any or all kinds of collaboration will be right for the task or the time.

We hope this book will bring different ways of collaborating alive for you and help you see some of the extraordinary collaborative practices that we have seen. We hope it will help acquaint you more deeply with the design elements of different ways of collaborating deliberately. We have tried to dig deeper into the cultures, networks, and systems that precede and surround these collaborative designs so that you can become more alert to and adept at transferring collaborative practices from one place to another. And, through the inspiring practices we have put before you, we hope you will be equally inspired to collaborate more effectively with those around you so that all your students will develop, grow, and succeed.

Andy Hargreaves
Boston College, December 2017

Acknowledgments

M any people have made this work possible and enabled us to bring it to fruition. First and foremost, we are grateful to the Qatar Foundation and its global outlook for funding and supporting the research and original report on which this book is based. We are also grateful to the classroom teachers, their students, school principals, and system-level leaders of the five schools and networks included in this book. They all eagerly responded to our requests to observe them in action and welcomed us with open arms—exemplifying the very spirit of collaborative professionalism that we had come to see.

Some key individuals supplied us with their expertise, networks, and generosity in enabling us to gain access to the various sites and to help us interpret what we were witnessing there: the faculty of education of Hong Kong University and Dr. Peng Liu in Hong Kong; Danette Parsley and Education Northwest in the U.S. Pacific Northwest; Juan Cristóbal García-Huidobro of Boston College and Vicky Colbert and Laura Vega with Escuela Nueva in Colombia; Yngve Lindvig and Anders Ruud Fosnaes in Norway; and former and present Boston College doctoral students Matt Welch and Shaneé Wangia in Ontario.

Some of our opening argument builds on a paper that we wrote as part of our preparation for this report. We are grateful to Emerald Publishing for permission to draw on our original article, which appears as the following in our references:

Hargreaves, A., & O'Connor, M. T. (2017). Cultures of professional collaboration: Their origins and opponents. *Journal of*

Professional Capital and Community, 2(2), 74–85. https://doi .org/10.1108/JPCC-02-2017-0004

Our principles of effective network development were first explored in a coauthored paper in the *Peabody Journal of Education*. This appears in our references as the following:

Hargreaves, A., Parsley, D., & Cox, E. (2015). Designing and launching rural school improvement networks: Aspirations and actualities. *Peabody Journal of Education, 90*(2), 306–321. https://doi.org/10.1080/0161956X.2015.1022391

We are also appreciative of our two WISE report reviewers, Amanda Datnow and Ann Lieberman; of the support of Muhammad Salman Bin Mohamed Khair, Asmaa Alfadala, and their colleagues at the WISE Foundation; and, not least, of the editorial support of Desirée Bartlett, Arnis Burvikovs, and the editorial staff of Corwin for making this book far better than we could have made it all by ourselves.

About the Authors

Andy Hargreaves is Research Professor at the Lynch School of Education at Boston College. He is president of the International Congress of School Effectiveness and Improvement, founding editor-in-chief of the *Journal of Professional Capital and Community*, and adviser in education to the premier of Ontario and the first minister of Scotland.

Andy has consulted with the Organisation for Economic Co-operation and Development, the World Bank, governments, universities, and teacher unions worldwide. Andy's more than 30 books have attracted multiple Outstanding Writing Awards— including the prestigious 2015 Grawemeyer Award in Education for *Professional Capital* (with Michael Fullan).

He has been honored with the 2016 Horace Mann Award in the United States and the Robert Owen Award in Scotland for services to public education. Andy has been ranked by *Education Week* in the top 10 scholars with most influence on the U.S. education policy debate. In 2015, Boston College gave him its Excellence in Teaching With Technology Award. He is a fellow of the Royal Society of Arts.

Michael T. O'Connor is the assistant director of the Providence Alliance for Catholic Teachers program at Providence College in Providence, Rhode Island, in the United States. In this role, Michael teaches master's-level courses, provides supervision and instructional coaching to the program's teachers, and offers support to the program's partner Catholic schools in the New England region. A former middle school English Language Arts (ELA) teacher and instructional coach, Michael received his PhD in curriculum and instruction with a focus in literacy from the Lynch School of Education at Boston College. While working on his doctorate, he worked with Andy Hargreaves and Dennis Shirley on the Northwest Rural Innovation and Student Engagement (NW RISE) network project, which included supporting the work of the ELA group. His dissertation explored secondary students' language choices in authentic, community-based writing activities and the ways in which teachers collaborated to support student writing across rural contexts.

PART I

Developing and Designing Collaborative Professionalism

CHAPTER
1

The Case for Collaborative Professionalism

FROM PROFESSIONAL COLLABORATION TO COLLABORATIVE PROFESSIONALISM

Collaboration is the new chorus line for innovation and improvement. The Organisation for Economic Co-operation and Development strongly promotes it, many teacher unions are behind it, and more and more governments are seeing the point of it. The evidence that, in general, professional collaboration benefits students and teachers alike has become almost irrefutable. Professional collaboration boosts student achievement, increases teacher retention, and enhances the implementation of innovation and change. The big questions are no longer about whether teachers *should* collaborate. No profession can serve people effectively if its members do not share and exchange knowledge about their expertise or about the clients, patients, or students they have in common. The big questions, rather, are about *how* and *how well* teachers and other educators collaborate. Not all kinds of collaboration are desirable or effective, and not all are appropriate for the people who practice it or for the task at hand.

Collaborative professionalism is a deeper and more rigorous form of professional collaboration. *Professional collaboration* refers to how people collaborate within a profession. That collaboration may be strong or weak, effective or ineffective, and undertaken one way or another. *Collaborative pro-fessionalism* is about how people collaborate more professionally and also how they work as a profession in a more collaborative way.

> No profession can serve people effectively if its members do not share and exchange knowledge about their expertise or about the clients, patients, or students they have in common.

Professional collaboration is descriptive—it delineates how people work together in a profession. *Collaborative professionalism* is normative—it is about creating stronger and better professional practice together.

The *professional* aspect of collaboration is about exercising good judgment, being committed to improvement, sharing and deepening expertise, and getting neither too close to nor too distant from the people the profession serves. The *collaborative* aspect of professionalism refers to how members of their profession labor or work together rather than only talk, share, and reflect together. In a capsule definition:

> Collaborative professionalism is about how teachers and other educators transform teaching and learning together to work with all students to develop fulfilling lives of meaning, purpose, and success. It is organized in an evidence-informed, but not data-driven, way through rigorous planning, deep and sometimes demanding dialogue, candid but constructive feedback, and continuous collaborative inquiry.

The joint work of collaborative professionalism is embedded in the culture and life of the school, where educators actively care for and have solidarity with each other as fellow professionals as they pursue their challenging work together and where they collaborate professionally in ways that are responsive to and inclusive of the cultures of their students, themselves, the community, and the society.

We make the case for collaborative professionalism through portrayals of deliberately designed professional collaboration in five different parts of the world (Hong Kong, the United States, Colombia, Norway, and Canada). This evidence leads us to set out 10 tenets of collaborative professionalism designs. We also outline four contextual and cultural factors (what we call the four *B*s) that are indispensable when attempting to initiate and implement these collaborative designs in schools or systems elsewhere.

DESIGNING COLLABORATIVE PROFESSIONALISM

How do schools, professional organizations, and school systems deliberately design ways in which teachers can work together? We went in search of collaborative designs that were widely known in different parts of the world. We chose sites on four continents to ensure that diverse systems and cultures were represented. We selected different designs of professional collaboration based on the message systems (the way that schools communicate what they do) that they mainly addressed—curriculum, pedagogy, evaluation, the whole school and its organization, and the relationship to the whole society.

Additionally, the collaboration had to involve groups of three or more educators who were participating within or beyond one specific school building. We also restricted our study to collaboration among education professionals, rather than ones that engaged other partners such as businesses or universities.

After visiting seven sites, we chose five systems that were sufficiently developed in having persisted for at least four years:

- Open class/lesson study: a Hong Kong secondary school
- Collaborative curriculum planning networks: a network of rural schools in the U.S. Pacific Northwest
- Cooperative learning and working: an elementary school in Norway
- Collaborative pedagogical transformation: the *Escuela Nueva* network of 25,000 schools in rural Colombia
- Professional learning communities (PLCs): remote school districts in Ontario, Canada, that serve aboriginal and other students

THE 10 TENETS OF COLLABORATIVE PROFESSIONALISM

Analysis of the case studies points to 10 tenets of collaborative professionalism that distinguish it from earlier versions of professional collaboration.

1. *Collective Autonomy.* Educators have more independence from top-down bureaucratic authority, but less independence from each other. Teachers are given or take authority.

2. *Collective Efficacy.* The belief that, together, we can make a difference to the students we teach, no matter what.

3. *Collaborative Inquiry (CI).* Teachers routinely explore problems, issues, or differences of practice together in order to improve or transform what they are doing. CI is embedded in the everyday work of teaching. Teachers inquire into problems before rushing into solving them.

4. *Collective Responsibility.* People have a mutual obligation to help each other and to serve the students they have in common. Collective responsibility is about *our* students, rather than *my* students.

5. *Collective Initiative.* In collaborative professionalism, there are fewer initiatives, but there is more initiative. Teachers step forward, and the system encourages it. Collaborative professionalism is about communities of strong individuals who are committed to helping and learning from each other.

6. *Mutual Dialogue.* Difficult conversations can be had and are actively instigated among educators. Feedback is honest. There is genuine dialogue about valued differences of opinion about ideas, curriculum materials, or the challenging behavior of students. Participants are often protected by protocols that insist on clarification and listening before any disagreement is brought forth.

7. *Joint Work.* Joint work exists in team teaching, collaborative planning, collaborative action research, providing structured feedback, undertaking peer reviews, discussing examples of student work, and so forth. Joint work involves actions and sometimes products or artifacts (such as a lesson, curriculum, or feedback report) and is often facilitated by structures, tools, and protocols.

8. *Common Meaning and Purpose.* Collaborative professionalism aspires to, articulates, and advances a common purpose that is greater than test scores or even academic achievement on its own. It addresses and engages with goals of education that enable and encourage young people to grow and flourish as whole human beings who can live lives and find work that has meaning and purpose for themselves and for society.

9. *Collaborating With Students.* In the deepest forms of collaborative professionalism, students are actively engaged with their teachers in constructing change together.

10. *Big-Picture Thinking for All.* In collaborative professionalism, everyone gets the big picture. They see it, live it, and create it together.

THE CULTURE AND CONTEXT OF COLLABORATIVE PROFESSIONALISM

Whenever a new method, practice, or protocol surfaces in education, there is a common tendency to spread it too far and too fast, with little thought as to what else may be needed for the particular model or design to be effective. When we are considering adapting collaborative designs from elsewhere, there are four *B*s of collaborative professionalism that can help us understand and also activate the contexts and cultures that precede, succeed, and surround it.

- What came *before* the model existed?
- What other kinds of collaboration exist *betwixt* or alongside it in the school and in the distinctive culture of the whole society?
- What connections does any specific design have to collaborative ideas and actions *beyond* the school, in overseas schools, in international research, in online interaction, or elsewhere?
- What support does the system provide *beside* the specific collaborative design in government grants, official allocations of time, or wider professional networks?

MOVING TOWARD COLLABORATIVE PROFESSIONALISM

Schools and systems have become more knowledgeable about how to shift from cultures of individualism to cultures of collaboration. But they have often pushed for the wrong kinds of collaboration in the wrong way. In collaborative professionalism, we want deeper collaboration in stronger relationships of trust, support, and solidarity. We also want more professionalism involving good data and good judgment, more candid and respectful professional

> Schools and systems have become more knowledgeable about how to shift from cultures of individualism to cultures of collaboration. But they have often pushed for the wrong kinds of collaboration in the wrong way.

dialogue, more thoughtful feedback, more collective responsibility for each other's results, and more courageous engagement with bolder visions of education that will help young people become change makers in their own and other people's lives.

MAKING IT HAPPEN

In the final chapter, we look at what practitioners, leaders, and policy-makers can specifically do to make collaborative professionalism happen through determining what should be stopped, what should continue, and what should be started for the first time.

WE RECOMMEND THAT EDUCATORS

- *stop investing too much in data teams at the expense of broader collaborative inquiry;*
- *stop importing unmodified alien designs from other countries and cultures;*
- *end high rates of educator turnover that destroy cohesive cultures;*
- *keep evolving the complexity of collaborative professionalism beyond conversations or meetings to deeper forms of dialogue, feedback, and inquiry;*
- *continue soliciting critical feedback from peers inside and outside one's own community;*
- *turn students into change makers with their teachers;*
- *adduce the added value of digital technology by carefully determining where and when it has a positive impact on collaborative professionalism; and*
- *build more collaboration across schools and systems, including and especially in broader environments of competition.*

In the past quarter century, teaching has made great strides in building more *professional collaboration*. It is now time for this to progress into *collaborative professionalism*, rooted in inquiry, responsive to feedback, and always up for a good argument. Are you a collaborative professional? Are you ready for this kind of challenge?

CHAPTER
2

Moving Toward Collaborative Professionalism

DEVELOPING COLLABORATIVE PROFESSIONALISM

"Many hands make light work."

"A trouble shared is a trouble halved."

"No man is an island, entire of itself."

Countless idioms testify to the value of teamwork and collaboration. Of course, there are also sayings to the contrary:

"If you want a job done, do it yourself."

"Too many cooks spoil the broth."

"Misery loves company."

Collaboration, community, and teamwork promise many benefits. These include greater efficiency, better results, moral consolation, enhanced motivation, commitment to change, worker retention, diversity of perspective, and tenacity in the face of obstacles or disappointments. A culture that works together also holds out the prospect of a longer-term impact that is not dependent on one or two talented individuals who may leave as quickly as they arrived. At the same time, collaboration can lead to groupthink, the evasion of personal responsibility, and the suppression of critical judgment. Teams can be used to implement the will of tyrants. Communities can become claustrophobic or controlling. Few people, anywhere, clamor for more meetings.

Every so often in education, the positive potential of collaboration comes into prominence. It may be seen as a way to rebuild motivation in and improve recruitment to a profession that has become dispirited by the excesses of accountability. It might be needed to achieve sophisticated learning goals, such as creativity and critical thinking that, unlike simple test score improvements, cannot be secured with prescription and compliance. It can be a way to galvanize massive collective efforts to bring about greater equity and inclusion by transforming their schools and communities. We live in a time when there is a great convergence among these things.

But we need to know more about the different ways that educators can and do collaborate, about how effective these various approaches are, and about how appropriate they are for the cultures that are adopting them and the purposes for which they are being employed. We need to know these things so that the teaching profession can become both more collaborative and more professional in order to have the best possible impact on all students and the future society.

In this book, you will encounter teachers who have built collaboration with each other by modeling it on the cooperative learning they have introduced to their students. You will see how teachers not only endure but expect and encourage other teachers to come into their classrooms and give them critical feedback on their practice. You will come across teachers who have collaborated with each other across thousands of miles in rural America by finding ways for their students to collaborate with one another. You will experience how teachers seized the running of professional learning communities (PLCs) from their principals. And you will discover how thousands of teachers in Latin America worked together with their students and each other to build peace and democracy after decades of drug wars in their country.

This is a book about teacher collaboration. But it is not about the clichés of how teachers talk, share, and learn from each other and need more time and support to do it. Nor is it about how teachers are put into teams to solve carefully specified problems through analysis of data in a few weeks or a year. Our book is about the hard but fulfilling work of collaboration that pervades some of the best cultures of teaching and connects the daily issues of students' learning and development to big questions of social transformation through learning and teaching that has meaning and purpose.

Collaborative professionalism is a paradoxical juxtaposition of two big ideas or movements: professions and labor. Historically, professions have been defined in terms of their autonomy. Labor unions, by contrast, have been defined by their solidarity. Whether teachers are professionals or laborers has been a long-running debate in education—not least among teachers themselves.[1] The point of collaborative professionalism is that the collaborative aspect is not directed only to defending pay and working conditions—though these also matter a lot—but also to working hard, laboring together with everyone's collective might, on behalf of all the students in a school, a district, or a nation.

One of the first definitions of *collaborative professionalism* emerged in Ontario, Canada, where one of us serves as an education advisor to Premier Kathleen Wynne. In 2014, the government of Ontario set out new goals for education that included broadly defined excellence, greater equity and inclusion, and enhanced well-being.[2] The new priorities called on all of the collective skills and capacities that teachers and other professionals could muster. In elementary schools, teachers who were unconfident in math would need to work closely with those who had greater expertise.

Classroom teachers would need to work alongside those with special education assignments. Addressing the risks to child well-being called for teachers to collaborate with mental health professionals. The educational system was coming out of a period of austerity, and relationships among all the partners in the system had to be rebuilt.

In response to these changes, the Ministry of Education and its partners set out "a vision for collaborative professionalism that improves student achievement and well-being."[3] It defined collaborative professionalism as

> [professionals at all levels] working together, sharing knowledge, skills, and experience to improve student achievement, and [the] well-being of both students and staff. . . . Collaborative professionalism values the voices of all and reflects an approach in support of our shared responsibility to provide equitable access to learning for all. All staff are valued and have a shared responsibility as they contribute to collaborative learning cultures.[4]

Not everyone was comfortable with this strategy of collaborative professionalism. Administrators feared they might lose their authority. Teachers were concerned it would be a way for principals to make them work together on unwanted priorities against their will. Through a lot of discussion and building of trust, most of these fears were dispelled.

The idea and strategy of collaborative professionalism was supported by thought leaders in Ontario education. Carol Campbell argued that complex learning outcomes required "an ecosystem of formal and informal leaders and learners . . . being enabled and equipped to learn together, to share their knowledge, to de-privatize practices, to innovate and to co-create improvements in professional knowledge, skills and practices."[5]

> Collaborative professionalism is about working well together in a professional way. It is hard work for a good cause, but it is not self-abnegating or joyless.

Lynn Sharratt said that collaborative professionalism meant school leaders would need to develop a genuinely shared vision with teachers and others.[6]

Michael Fullan and Andy Hargreaves argue that collaborative professionalism should be a culture that permeates the whole school or system, not simply a set of meetings or task-driven teams. It should promote "regular quality feedback related to improvement."[7] It should explicitly contribute to the improvement of the wider society. In collaborative professionalism, "everyone is involved: no exceptions." There is enjoyment as well as impact, better time as well as more time. There is diversity and disagreement in a culture that values the individual as part of the collective. Lastly, there is collective responsibility for other people's impact on their students as well as personal responsibility for teachers' impact on students of their own. The school is no longer about *my* students. It is about *our* students. Collaborative professionalism certainly entails sharing, talking, trusting, co-creating, and learning. But it also values other verbs, such as challenging, critiquing, including, empowering, and debating.

Collaborative professionalism is about working well together in a professional way. It is hard work for a good cause, but it is not self-abnegating or joyless. Collaborative professionalism makes teaching more interesting and engaging for everyone who is involved in it. Our book addresses these and other aspects of collaborative professionalism through five global examples.

DESIGNING COLLABORATION

Professional collaboration today can be strong or weak, too comfortable or too contrived. With such variation in quality and impact, even if the average impact is positive, vulnerability to external critique is still substantial. The time has come, therefore, to remove the bad variation in *professional collaboration*. It is time to move from the high variability of professional collaboration to the more consistent high quality in *collaborative professionalism*.

The next big question, then, is what's the best way to collaborate? What designs are out there and how should educators choose between them? What else do schools need as well as a good design or protocol? How will working collaboratively fit into the wider culture or community? What's best? What's next?

This is the focus of our next chapter, which will take us into five designs in different schools and systems. Here, we will see collaborative professionalism is manifested in very different cultures and contexts, yet in ways that express a common set of inspiring and impactful principles.

How do teachers collaborate? How do schools, professional organizations, and school systems deliberately design ways in which teachers can work together? How can a school choose a design on some principled basis, other than from a list of options, because of what their system requires them to do or as a result of what they have encountered most recently in a professional development workshop?

The British educational theorist Basil Bernstein argued that in schools, formal educational knowledge was realized through three message systems that conveyed what was important for students to learn.[8] They were as follows:

- *curriculum*—which defines what counts as valid knowledge
- *pedagogy*—which defines what counts as valid transmission of knowledge
- *evaluation*—which defines what counts as valid realization of this knowledge on the part of the taught

One way of classifying collaborative practices is to see what they focus on in relation to these message systems. If they concentrate on curriculum, then they may take the form of collaborative curriculum planning or review. If they focus on pedagogy and pedagogical transformation, they might concentrate on culturally responsive pedagogy or cooperative learning strategies, for example. And if they concentrate on evaluation, they might bring teachers together to undertake moderated marking or grading, participate in quality reviews of each other's schools or districts, or develop and review portfolio or performance assessments together.

These categories are not watertight. Networks that bring together teachers of writing, for example, address issues of curriculum and pedagogy together.[9] Lesson study seems to be mainly about pedagogy, but also entails reviewing curriculum workbooks and other materials. But pinpointing where the prime focus of collaboration is in relation to these three message systems is a useful way to think about where to start or go next on its collaborative journey.

In addition, there are at least two more message systems. One is the whole school and its organization and direction.[10] Engaging staff in the vision of the school is an example of this. So is the practice of schools assisting other schools to help them improve their performance. Another message system is the whole society, its development, and how student learning contributes to this.[11]

With these considerations in mind, we set out a provisional chart of our five cases as examples of practices of collaborative professionalism (Figure 2.1). The chart consists of the following cases:

- *Open class/lesson study*: a Hong Kong secondary school, part of a network of 20, that has designed and developed its own version of lesson study under the name *open class*

- *Collaborative curriculum planning networks*: a 4-year-old evolving network of 27 districts across four states in the U.S. Pacific Northwest that engages teachers in "job-alike" groups for collaborative planning of curriculum units

- *Cooperative learning and working*: a school in southern Norway that uses cooperative learning principles among its teachers as well as its students

- *Collaborative pedagogical transformation*: the *Escuela Nueva* network of 25,000 schools that bases teacher collaboration on student collaboration and transformative pedagogy in rural Colombia to promote peace, well-being, and democracy

- *Professional learning communities (PLCs)*: one of the most remote school districts in Ontario, Canada, that serves large proportions of aboriginal students and that has moved to embrace teacher-led PLCs

Figure 2.1 Cases by collaborative design, context, and message systems.

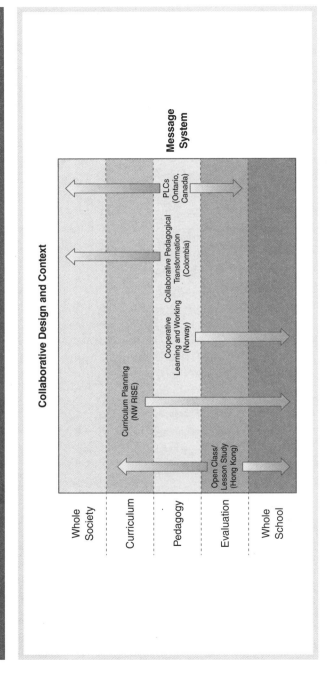

Collaborative Design and Context

Message System

The five schools and systems were selected for several reasons:

1. Their *distribution on the figure*: The arrows on the chart show how the focus of each case of collaboration expanded and developed over time.

2. *Representation of a range of diverse cultures* and systems on four continents, rather than being confined to a single culture that might then be hard to transfer to other schools, cultures, and systems

3. *Relationship to a wider system* such as a network, district, or government policy framework that enables us to understand how collaboration in schools is enabled or supported by a wider system

4. *Evolution and persistence* over at least 4 years, so that the collaborative practices are more mature and less likely to fade away

5. *Fit with our emerging sense of collaborative professionalism*: We deliberately did not choose some designs (such as data teams) as self-contained initiatives because analysis of data by teachers works best when it is part of a broader process of collaborative inquiry, interpretation, and professional judgment.[12]

What we will see next are examples not of teachers talking about or remembering their experiences of collaboration, but actually collaborating. We will see that teachers collaborate in rich countries and poor countries, in cities and in remote villages and small towns. We will learn how collaboration was deliberately designed and redesigned over time, how it came to be, and what it was like beforehand. We will see collaboration go beyond talk, beyond data, and beyond meetings and teams to become part of the life of schools and how they operate. It's time to look at collaborative professionalism up close and in action.

NOTES

1. The classic article on this question is Ginsburg, M., Meyenn, R., & Miller, H. (1980). Teachers' conceptions of professionalism and trades unionism:

An ideological analysis. In P. Woods (Ed.), *Teacher strategies* (pp. 178–212). London, UK: Croom Helm.

2. Ontario Ministry of Education. (2014). *Achieving excellence*. Retrieved from http://www.edu.gov.on.ca/eng/about/great.html

3. As quoted in Section C. 2.5 of the Teacher/Occasional Teacher Central Agreement between the Ontario Government and the Elementary Teachers' Federation of Ontario, May 2015.

4. Ontario Ministry of Education. (2016). *Collaborative professionalism* (Policy/Program Memorandum No. 159). Toronto, Ontario: Author.

5. Campbell, C. (2016). Collaborative professionalism: Of, by and for Catholic school leaders. *Principal Connections, 20*(1), 6–7.

6. Sharratt, L. (2016). Setting the table for collaborative professionalism. *Principal Connections, 20*(1), 34–37.

7. Fullan, M., & Hargreaves, A. (2016). *Bringing the profession back in: Call to action.* Oxford, OH: Learning Forward. Retrieved from https://learningforward.org/docs/default-source/pdf/bringing-the-profession-back-in.pdf

8. Bernstein, B. (1971). On the classification and framing of educational knowledge. In M. F. D. Young (Ed.), *Knowledge and control* (pp. 47–69; p. 47). London, UK: Collier-MacMillan.

9. Lieberman, A., & Wood, D. (2002). The national writing project. *Educational Leadership, 59*(6), 40–43.

10. Bernstein, B. (1990). *The structuring of pedagogic discourse, Volume IV: Class, codes and control.* London, UK: Routledge.

11. Hargreaves, A., & Ainscow, M. (2015). The top and bottom of leadership and change. *Phi Delta Kappan, 97*(3), 42–48; Hargreaves, A., & Shirley, D. (2012). *The global fourth way: The quest for educational excellence.* Thousand Oaks, CA: Corwin; Munby, S., & Fullan, M. (2016). *Inside-out and downside-up: How leading from the middle has the power to transform education systems.* Education Development Trust. Retrieved from https://michaelfullan.ca/wp-content/uploads/2016/02/Global-Dialogue-Thinkpiece.pdf

12. Datnow, A., & Park, V. (2014). *Data-driven leadership.* San Francisco, CA: Jossey-Bass; Hargreaves, A., & Braun, H. (2013, October 22). Six principles for using data to hold people accountable. *Washington Post.* Retrieved from http://www.washingtonpost.com/blogs/answer-sheet/wp/2013/10/22/six-principles-for-using-data-to-hold-people-accountable/; Hubers, M. D., Poortman, C. L., Schildkamp, K., Pieters, J. M., & Handelzalts, A. (2016). Opening the black box: Knowledge creation in data teams. *Journal of Professional Capital and Community, 1*(1), 41–68.

CHAPTER
3

Open Class and Lesson Study

Why do many teachers prefer to be left alone with their own classes? One of the most common explanations is that they don't like to be observed or evaluated.[1] Sometimes, it has been said, this is because they have little confidence or even false confidence in what they are doing or because the complexity of what is behind anyone's teaching cannot be picked up in a passing visit. So teaching in front of other teachers, when children can act out and plans can go awry, can make teachers vulnerable to the prospect of upsetting criticism.[2]

In systems where your pay or your job can depend on evaluations from a principal who might otherwise never come into your class, feedback can often seem intrusive and harsh. Equally, principals can overcompensate for this worry by giving teachers comments that are too bland or insufficiently incisive. The consequence in many schools is that everyone gets anxious, but little improves. Yet John Hattie points out that giving teachers feedback on their teaching has one of the highest effect sizes on student learning.[3]

Effective feedback is critical to improving teaching and learning, but teachers don't welcome feedback that feels episodic, arbitrary, or unfair. What is the way out of this conundrum?

One option that started out in Asia is known variously as *lesson study* or *learning study*. At Fanling Kau Yan College—a secondary school with over 700 students on the outskirts of Hong Kong, near the border with mainland China—they call it *open class*.

OPEN CLASS TEACHING

Welcome to Iris's eighth-grade English class at Fanling. Fanling is a government-subsidized school with a Christian foundation. As Principal Veronica Yau explained, many of its students come from surrounding neighborhoods where many "grassroots" families have "financial difficulties" and where some people have never traveled the 40 minutes or so by transit into the city center.[4] Because of the school's reputation as a successful school—it scores in the top 20% of schools making the most improvement based on the English language proficiency of their entering students—some of its students also come across the border from the mainland every day.

The school is nothing fancy architecturally or technologically. Like many other Hong Kong schools, in a city short on space, Fanling extends upward across multiple floors—seven, in its case. Fanling is a good school. Its teachers are very dedicated, and they work incredibly hard. The principal has to insist that teachers leave the school no later than 7:00 p.m. And in Iris's class, all this hard work shows.

Iris is teaching her students how to write a formal e-mail to a professional—the school's social worker—about a personal adolescent problem. This objective is a required part of the Hong Kong English language curriculum. With her class of over 30 students, Iris's lesson consists of several precisely timed and sequenced components, and it moves at a blistering pace. One of Fanling's prime areas of focus is developing students' ability to engage in self-regulated learning (SRL). As teachers in the school explain it, "If students fail, it's not because they don't want to learn but because they don't know what to do." This approach requires sophisticated lesson structures and supports and high levels of teacher skill.

Based on the work of Barry Zimmerman and Dale Schunck,[5] SRL at Fanling means getting students to take individual and shared responsibility for their learning, to reflect on and give one another feedback on that learning, and to regulate and monitor their own emotional behaviors in the classroom while they learn. Instead of traditional three-part lessons, since SRL was introduced into the first year of secondary school 5 years ago, a lot of the learning has been organized into eight steps or processes in which students have to demonstrate what they have been learning in real time. All in about 50 minutes! The eight steps are presented in Figure 3.1.[6]

The lesson is a combination of guided learning from the teacher, self-learning for each individual student, peer learning of students from each other, and shared learning as a whole class.

What does this look like in Iris's class? Iris begins by clearly setting out the objectives for the lesson. They comprise the nature and language structures of a formal e-mail explaining a problem with effects on feelings and then expressing this in students' own

Figure 3.1 The eight steps of SRL at Fanling.

1. **State and share objectives.**
2. **Guide the learning to follow.**
3. **Discuss in student pairs or groups.**
4. **Show what they have been learning on a small chalkboard.**
5. **Present this to each other and the class.**
6. **Get public teacher and class feedback.**
7. **Test what has been learned through worksheet exercises or iBoard demonstrations.**
8. **Conclude the lesson.**

formal e-mails and getting feedback on them from peers. The problem that is presented is a common one for adolescents everywhere—acne and body image issues that lead young people to experience self-consciousness and embarrassment. Iris displays the issue on her digital whiteboard and shows some positive and negative exemplars of how students might try to communicate this to their counselor. Iris is trying to ensure that students know what they have to do.

Students then quickly pair off to discuss what they see and to come up with some issues of their own that worry them in adolescence. They also have workbooks with questions to help them. The assigned time for discussion is very short—20 seconds! Interaction is focused and precise. Iris then has some interaction with the whole class. Some of the students jump to attention and raise their hands enthusiastically. "Let me try, let me try," they say—a common protocol for question-and-answer sessions in the school. There is another quick moment of sharing among students without referring to their workbooks—1 minute this time.

The class then quickly forms itself into prearranged mixed-ability groups designated by numbers and letters. They get out what they call their *iBoards* (small chalkboards that can be written on by a team) to write down how they would structure a formal e-mail about an actual adolescent problem (such as name-calling or mood swings) that has been experienced by one of the group members.

In the next stage of the lesson, students hang up their iBoards on hooks at the front of the class so everyone can see them. Iris then asks for two group leaders to volunteer to present what is on their iBoard to the rest of the class. "Let me try," they say again. The students make their presentations and engage in some more whole-class interaction, then Iris goes back to the whiteboard to draw some final conclusions about the characteristics of a formal e-mail and closes the lesson.

The whole lesson flies by. It's a whirlwind of orchestrated activity. The strategies are a sophisticated combination of U.S.-style cooperative learning and a range of methods with more direct instruction. All this occurs under the supervision and guidance of a teacher who has absolute command and authority in her class, where nobody can let his or her attention wander for a second. This is impressive enough. The really remarkable thing, though, is that Iris is teaching this complex class in front of a dozen or so visitors!

OPEN CLASS FEEDBACK

Every year, on two occasions, Fanling opens around half of its classes to outside visitors—up to 100 or more of them. It's what the school calls *open class*. On the day Iris was teaching her class about formal e-mails, she and 27 colleagues were teaching in front of principals from other schools, as well as teachers who had been sent there from other parts of Hong Kong by their own principals. This situation would be scary enough for any teacher—a dozen observers instead of only one or two and a sophisticated and demanding lesson structure that could easily get derailed at any moment. But there is also something else: Once the class is over and the students leave, there is a post–open class conference, where visiting professionals are invited to give their feedback to Iris.

Some of the feedback was complimentary: The objectives and structure were very clear; there was lots of peer learning. More than a bit of the feedback was also unambiguously critical. Why did the teacher only call on a small number of students to volunteer answers? Was the pace of the lesson too fast for some students? Suppose they didn't understand everything that took place and started to fall behind. What would the teacher do then? The lesson was brisk, but don't there also need to be quiet moments when the teacher can tap into what her students are thinking? And what about the shy student whose presentation of her group's iBoard results to the whole class was barely audible?

This is a lot of criticism for any teacher to endure, especially in public. Some teachers at Fanling remember all too well what it felt like being observed when they were in other schools or earlier in their career. One said that when she was "very green," she "got very upset about feedback." However, Fanling's open class has very specific protocols that make teachers less vulnerable while also enhancing the quality of professional learning for the visitors and themselves.

First, the purpose and objectives of open class are made very clear when Principal Yau addresses all the visitors in an open assembly at the start of the day. Marco, the senior teacher leader, then reinforces the message with a PowerPoint presentation on their open class procedures to the visitors who have come to the English class. He sets out three purposes of the open class—to foster professional growth through reflection on the lessons observed, to improve learning and teaching together, and to refine SRL lessons through the collective wisdom of all participants. He then presents five essential principles and protocols of constructive professional feedback to guide the observers (see Figure 3.2).

These principles and protocols mean that observers will be less inclined to make vague, general judgments or personally upsetting comments about what they think is good or poor teaching. The feedback is facilitated. No single person or point of view will dominate. The feedback will be neither too blunt nor too bland. Observers are directed to focus not on the personality of the teacher but on the task he or she is performing. Marco and Iris try to ensure this by running the post-conference in a carefully structured way, similar to one of their classes. They divide the observers into groups—one concentrating on the objectives and the learning guides or workbooks, the other focusing on teaching strategies and student participation. Each group also has their own iBoard and writes down four key ideas. The visitors are very engaged with the task and hang up their iBoards when they have finished, just like the students. Then they move into whole-group feedback.

Figure 3.2 Fanling's five essential principles and protocols of constructive professional feedback.

- Mutual respect
- Equal participation
- Focusing on self-regulated learning (SRL)
- Understanding the limitations of the teacher and the characteristics of the school
- Sincere and honest sharing of inspiration and suggestions

The structure focuses and depersonalizes the feedback, and both Iris and Marco respond with openness and authenticity. Iris isn't stoic about accepting criticism. She

> Principles and protocols mean that observers will be less inclined to make vague, general judgments or personally upsetting comments about what they think is good or poor teaching.

and her colleagues at Fanling actively encourage and directly solicit it. Iris accepts that it is easy to omit quiet students when others are so eager to respond. Marco explains how concentrating too much on formal grammar and vocabulary can limit other aspects of students' thinking. Visitors also hear how many students are able to keep up with the pace because they have practiced and read aloud key parts of the vocabulary beforehand in afternoon preparation sessions. Everyone is learning. They "share what they can learn from the visitors and celebrate the learning together."

OPEN CLASS PLANNING

It's not only the protocols that create a positive feedback process, though. There's also the fact that this lesson is not Iris's lesson. At least, it's not *only* Iris's lesson. Marco has taught it. So have several colleagues in her department. The lesson belongs to all of them. They created and revised it together. They rehearsed and then reviewed an earlier version of the lesson together the previous week. Iris and her departmental team then prepared the lesson the day before open class. They discussed content issues, such as appropriate vocabulary and avoiding grammatical contractions. They reviewed the slide presentation for the visitors. Grace, the head of the English department, made suggestions about how different iBoard groups could focus on feelings, language, and other issues, respectively. The lesson is a common product and responsibility. The successes and limitations belong to all of them. In Principal Yau's words, "No one is perfect, but the team can be."

All these processes apply to other subjects and teachers, too. Every teacher teaches an open class at least once a year. Parents considering sending their children to the school are invited to open classes as well. On the same day Iris was teaching her English class, Candy, the head of the science department, was doing an open class on energy transfer. As in the case of the English lesson, there were many components to this class. There were two teachers in the large class, rotating who was responsible for supervising simultaneous lab experiments. Magnesium strips were lit over Bunsen burners and paper balloons rose with the hot air. A student with severe visual impairment pushed a toy truck down a ramp. Another child blew air into a wind instrument to create sound vibration. Students and their teachers discussed thermal energy, sound energy, potential energy, and kinetic energy. As in Iris's class, students watched their teacher lead lab demonstrations. They got out their iBoards and worked in pairs, small groups, as a class, and individually as they filled out answers in their workbooks (Figure 3.3).

Like Iris, this was not the teacher's own lesson either. The day before open class, we joined Candy and a team of three other science teachers in a planning meeting for this lesson. All of them had taught the lesson before and were now reviewing what they

Figure 3.3 Students working on their iBoards.

experienced and what they would change. At first, they talked about logistical issues, such as the setup of the room, time management, and the different pace at which each of them moved. Then they explored technical vocabulary and the language of the workbook. From this, they started to imagine and reflect on how students experienced the lesson, and they delved deeper into their own understandings and interpretations of their subject matter knowledge. Is it appropriate to say that hot air pushes a turbine, one of them speculated, if it is actually particles that are creating the movement? The teachers were excited. They were, as adults and intellectuals, engaging with high-level understandings of their own subject. Through this, they now also realized how difficult it must be for their students to distinguish between moving air and energy conversion. How deeply do students need to understand the nature of particles, they wondered. Describing what they are learning about energy conversion, in writing on their iBoards, would make students' understanding more visible, the teachers decided.

So, the secrets of open class are in its *purpose* of shared professional learning and improvement, in the *structure* of protocols and planning procedures, and in the *culture* of shared ownership and responsibility. Educators at Fanling believe that all this work is having a positive impact on their students. Talking together, Iris and Candy note how, since implementing SRL and open class feedback, student engagement has increased. They no longer have students who do not really enjoy coming to school. There are far fewer discipline problems of students in class such as "sleeping, getting mad, or not being on task." "When students work together," one of them said, "they have collective responsibility and don't let feelings get in the way."

Assessment results determined by the Hong Kong Bureau of Education have also improved—for instance, by 10% in English over 3 years. However, Principal Yau tells teachers, "Don't worry about achievement results. Just improve the classroom atmosphere." "We are not doing this to boost up results," she emphasizes, "otherwise teachers will be very stressed." Principal Yau and her staff believe that when they change the teaching, the results will also change.

LESSON STUDY

Fanling's particular approach to the open class method is unique, yet also part of a wider tradition in Asia and elsewhere of using precise collaborative methods to improve teaching and learning. These came to prominent attention in the West when, in the 1990s, in the days before the first Organisation for Economic Co-operation and Development (OECD) Program for International Student Assessment (PISA) test results of educational performance were released, Japan topped the international rankings on the Third International Maths and Science Studies (TIMMS). A book by Stigler and Hiebert[7] drew attention to a phenomenon that they expressed in English as *lesson study*. In Japan, they explained, there had been a long tradition—more than a century—of teachers observing each other's lessons. This had evolved into a precise methodology of presentation, observation, inquiry, review, and implementation by groups of teachers within and across schools. Described by Stigler and Hiebert, these steps have parallels to those used at Fanling: defining and researching a problem that will be the focus of a lesson, planning the lesson, teaching it, observing it, reflecting on its effects, revising the lesson, teaching and observing the revised lesson, evaluating and reflecting a second time, then finally sharing the results.[8] Essentially, the lesson is a research lesson—a point of collaborative inquiry, action, and improvement.

Catherine Lewis of Mills College in California worked with a group of researchers to bring lesson study practices to the United States—expanding to hundreds of schools—and claimed positive effects on teacher development, including building a more collaborative culture in schools.[9] Lesson study spread to other countries such as Singapore, there is an international journal of learning and lesson study as well as an extensive research literature on the topic, and the World Association of Lesson Study now brings together researchers and practitioners from all over the world.[10]

A variant of lesson study more specific to Hong Kong is *learning study*.[11] Based on the work of Swedish researcher Ference Marton,[12] Hong Kong specialist Lo Mun Ling,[13] and one of the founders of

UK action research, John Elliott,[14] learning study concentrates more precisely on the phenomenon of learning (as opposed to issues such as behavior management) and applies much stricter research procedures to the study process.

The clear protocols and procedures of lesson study drew many Westerners to it. They regarded it as something that could develop or deepen ways for teachers to observe and evaluate each other's practice in schools and to break down the walls of professional isolation. But as Lewis warned in an early paper, lesson study techniques and procedures could not be properly understood without also understanding the culture and context in which they were used.[15] You couldn't take lesson study practices and directly transpose them to or impose them on Western classrooms. "The graveyards of U.S. educational reform are littered with once-promising innovations that were poorly understood, superficially implemented, and consequently pronounced ineffective," she warned.[16]

Japanese teachers, Lewis pointed out, already possessed a strong history and culture of collaboration in which teachers plan and talk together in common workrooms and everyone gets involved in social activities, hiking trips, sports events, and so on. Unlike Americans, Lewis added, Japanese teachers and Japanese people in general also approach feedback and criticism as spurs to further improvement and believe that, similar to student achievement, their own improvement will come about through collective effort. Japanese self-improvement, says Lewis, is almost a national religion. Lastly, in Japan—and unlike many U.S. jurisdictions—lesson study occurs within a climate where observations are not used to produce quick gains in achievement scores but to develop the whole child and his or her character.

The same considerations apply at Fanling. It's not only the practices and protocols of open class alone that explain its success. Open class, similar to other technical procedures for collaboration such as data teams, also depends for its success on a set of surrounding factors that cannot be captured completely in a set of steps and procedures.

THE FOUR *B*s OF COLLABORATIVE PROFESSIONALISM

Aside from the technical designs of professional collaboration, there are four sets of factors that affect how impactful or effective these designs might be. These are what we call the four *B*s of collaborative professionalism (see Figure 3.4).

1. Before

An iron and ironic rule of educational innovation is that an innovation effort is more likely to be successful if the school has already had experiences of innovating before. The same is true of collaboration. A new structure or protocol of collaboration such as data teams, peer review, or lesson study is more likely to be successful if people in the school already have previous experiences of working well together.[17]

> A new structure or protocol of collaboration such as data teams, peer review, or lesson study is more likely to be successful if people in the school already have previous experiences of working well together.

Candy, the head of the science department, had been at Fanling for 12 years. There has been a "paradigm shift" since she came, she said. At first, "there wasn't much interaction between students and teachers" or among teachers themselves. With Principal Yau's arrival 9 years ago, things began to change. Teachers were encouraged to collaborate much more, and the school became known for doing so.

Figure 3.4 The four *Bs* of deep collaboration.

Before. How did the school build collaboration *before* open class?

Betwixt. What other sorts of collaboration exist *alongside* open class?

Beyond. How does the school connect to ideas *beyond* open class?

Beside. What does the policy system wrap *around* open class?

A teacher who had been a vice principal in a previous school noted how "three Chinese history teachers [teaching there] taught alone and didn't share materials." At Fanling, however, "collaboration has always been a way of living." The nature of the collaboration had changed, though. Since SRL, Grace explained, although "teachers used to collaborate, it was informal and there was no special time or platform. Now it is more focused." Marco commented that while he had collaborated before in other schools, Fanling now put the "focus on how they learn together as teachers more." If anyone wants to look at the portability of a collaborative practice, it's important to consider the evolution that took place before it.

2. Betwixt

Fanling's collaborative focus on improving SRL through open class planning, review, and feedback doesn't happen in isolation. It doesn't occur in a culture where teachers work alone the rest of the time. In meetings, attention never wanders. Discussions are direct and precise. Referring to Hong Kong in general, as well as the school, Marco commented that "in this culture, time is precious. Every minute matters." There's no wandering around the topic or getting off the point. There is no idle chatter—until, that is, there are meals or social events, where everyone knows exactly how to relax and get to know each other as people.

Principal Yau and her team choose new recruits to the school carefully, based on their dedication to the students, their willingness to learn, and their ability to work in a team. They recruit "by heart— by *heart*," she repeats, clutching her chest. All teachers are involved in recruiting new teachers and present their shortlists to the board. Instead of requiring applicants to teach a sample lesson, which would, in their view, be artificial, as the teacher would have no relationship with the students, candidates are asked to observe other teachers' classes and give reflective feedback on them as if it were an open class. They are then invited to write a letter back to Marco on how the class could be improved. This way, the applicants learn what the school is like, how being observed is normal, and what the benefits of it can be. At the same time, the staff realize that "if they like to work individually, they may not be the person you are looking for."

"One flame is not enough," Principal Yau stresses.

The school isn't looking for new recruits who will comply with what the group requires. They are "looking for people who take initiative and come up with new ideas, for someone willing to share their ideas proactively." For instance, Jeffrey, a new teacher, was invited to lead other teachers on their use of technology. Marco, meanwhile, reflects that not only does he mentor new teachers, they also give him feedback that helps him improve his own classroom management skills.

Another of Fanling's teachers had gone to three schools when he was training. In other schools, he said, "some teachers like to work alone." At Fanling, though, he "knew the culture was collaborative. [You] could express opinions and listen to ideas even if [you] are new and feel very welcomed by everyone." The school gives you "so many chances to carry big projects even as a new member." He has already conducted workshops for them, including carrying out a demonstration lesson of his own. In other schools, he "would not be welcome to say anything," but at Fanling, he knows that when he says something, it "will be beneficial to other teachers as well."

There is one more dimension to the culture of collaboration that surrounds the open class version of lesson study at Fanling. It is culture in the wider sense—the distinctive culture of a country and community. Accompanying us on our visit to Fanling was Dr. Peng Liu from Hong Kong University. Dr. Liu is an expert on Chinese culture and its impact on education. Understanding professional relationships in Hong Kong means understanding the convergences between British colonial and Chinese culture. British colonial culture has left a legacy of examination competition and status, of selection and quality, and of formality in professional relations. It has also bequeathed the importance of the English language that used to be the language of instruction before Hong Kong's handover from Britain to China in 1997 and is still required in two secondary school subjects. At Fanling, these are English and science.

Then there is the considerable complexity of modern Chinese culture itself. Dr. Liu explains that this culture comprises elements that include, but are not restricted to, Confucianism, communism or socialism, market capitalism, and a range of religious and spiritual influences such as Taoism, Buddhism, and—in Hong Kong, including at Fanling itself—a range of Christian traditions.[18]

In his brief summary of Confucianism, Dr. Liu describes the centrality of five moral virtues: benevolence (the cultivation of feelings of respect, empathy, compassion, and love for all humanity), righteousness (just and appropriate conduct as part of the obligation to work for universal human well-being), propriety (in terms of proper conduct in relationships within families, among friends, and between leaders and followers), wisdom (the capacity to judge between right and wrong), and honesty (integrity and consistency between thoughts and deeds).

In addition to these virtues, conduct within Confucianism is governed by the importance of learning as a way of socializing people; collectivism in terms of the importance of the family, the group, the nation, and the company; and harmony of relationships. In addition, traditions of filial piety have translated into paternalistic or maternalistic forms of leadership—though these are being broken down by significant generational changes among the young who live in a global environment of consumer culture and access to the Internet. Last, *guanxi* or networks of reciprocity tie people together in family, commercial, and professional relationships.

Several spiritual traditions also support going with the natural flow of events and leading in a modest and introverted way (Taoism); enduring pain, embracing peace, and avoiding arrogance (Buddhism); and acting with integrity in caring relationships that serve others (Christianity).

The result at Fanling is what Dr. Liu calls *coordinated collaboration*. People participate and even initiate ideas in a culture of continuous learning as a way to support growth. They value and are committed to their professional community. They work hard, sacrifice, and are dedicated. They also respect the rules of hierarchy. At Fanling, when Principal Yau sits with Marco on one side and Grace (the head of the English department) on the other, they all participate, but she clearly cues the appropriate moment for the others to contribute. Everyone understands there are clear lines and distributions of responsibility. In meetings, there are no side conversations or interruptions. No one scrolls through their smartphones or answers e-mails on their laptops. Children stand when they answer questions or form cooperative groups. Guests are treated with honor. Gifts and thank-you cards are obligatory.

It is impossible to understand the nature of open class, lesson study, or learning study in Hong Kong, Chinese, or Southeast Asian cultures generally without also understanding all of this. This does not make Fanling's culture of collaboration better or worse than ones in the Untied States, United Kingdom, Latin America, the Middle East, or other societies. But it does mean we have to work very hard to figure out what needs to be done when a particular design for collaboration is moved from one system to another.

3. Beyond

A school will not progress as well as it can if its teachers only collaborate with each other. A disappointing feature of U.S. and other school systems is that they often discourage travel by educators to learn from systems outside their own country. In this respect, U.S. systems too often act like underperforming schools, as if they believe they have little to learn from anyone else and that cross-border and overseas visits are wasteful junkets paid for with taxpayer dollars. False confidence and un-Confucian arrogance become their undoing.

By comparison, Fanling educators constantly seek inspiration, evidence, and interaction from educators and researchers elsewhere. The initial idea of open class, in fact, came from connecting with Tokyo University's esteemed professor Manabu Sato, an international expert on learning communities.[19] Iris and Candy discussed how they deepened Fanling's approach to lesson study 5 years ago after they visited schools in Singapore—a nation that is itself extremely active in supporting professional intervisitation.[20] The Fanling team visited four schools that "did cycles of the same lesson over and over again to improve it." They "found it inspiring to keep working on the same lesson." Moreover, they learned, "the teacher conducting the lesson wasn't doing it with the teacher's class." When they returned, they began to make Fanling's approach to open class more structured.

In Hong Kong itself, Fanling has initiated and led a network of 20 other schools—5% of all the schools—in using open class methods in an annual festival to which they invite members of the government education bureau. This influences the system that influences them.

Last, many teachers, especially younger ones like their peers in other Asian countries such as South Korea, share what they are doing enthusiastically on the Internet.[21] Fanling's teachers take smartphone photographs from their lessons and share them on the application WhatsApp. They send up to 20 snapshots a day of PowerPoint slides or things on the blackboard. Their principal can also see these, which helps her stay connected to what they are doing. Whether it is through international visits, local network building, or digital platforms, Fanling teachers are eager gatherers and disseminators of ideas that have impact for their practice.

4. Beside

In most cases, if we want to understand schools, we must also understand the systems they are in. Hong Kong has not always supported professional collaboration and educational innovation. In the mid-1990s, the city's education system was highly didactic, and many teachers could not instruct students effectively in the required language of English. In a few short years, after the transfer of political authority from London to Beijing, Hong Kong education has risen into the top 10 of the OECD PISA rankings. It realized that with the new availability of mainland Chinese low-cost labor nearby, its own citizens would need to be educated to much higher standards of skill.[22]

The Hong Kong government sent ministry delegations overseas.[23] The teaching focus moved toward active learning, education for understanding, demonstrations of learning in practice, and wider life learning outside of school that was connected to real-world environments.[24] But none of this would have taken off without appropriate professional development or strategies to circulate good practices and move them around. The former head of the Education Bureau had disapproved of the top-down approach to centralized curriculum reform in the United Kingdom, so Hong Kong searched for a more professionally inclusive approach to change instead.

In her last few days in office, Hong Kong's Education Bureau Chief, KK Chan, explained some of the changes that the system had made since 2002 to strengthen the teaching profession and get it to work together more collaboratively:[25]

- *Government-funded collaborative projects* with research and development elements
- *University–school partnership projects* that cover diverse topics from whole-school approaches, curriculum planning, pedagogy, assessment, literacy, e-learning, and values education
- *Secondment (temporary transfer) of teachers and principals* to government and the university to nurture leaders in schools, consolidate and share networks, and transfer knowledge for different themes across the schools. "Schools were not happy at first because they lost good teachers," Ms. Chan explained, but they "persuaded them that this is was a tribute to how good they were in developing people for the government and university."
- *School-based professional collaboration* through promotion of collaborative lesson planning, peer observations, and staff development days. Processes such as peer observation, she pointed out, were outstanding in mainland China. According to OECD data, peer review in Hong Kong in eighth-grade mathematics and science increased by more than 25% between 2003 and 2011.[26]
- *Creation of curriculum leadership positions* in primary schools
- *Learning from other systems* by organizing visits to high-performing systems in mainland China and Ontario, Canada, for example

Many of the resources for this work go on grants in 3-year cycles, generating considerable investment and energy for change across the system. Hong Kong is not a perfect system. It does not perform as well on educational equity or child well-being as it does on overall educational achievement.[27] However, the Hong Kong Education Bureau has avoided making detailed top-down mandates and has provided support, incentives, encouragement, and freedom for professionals to set directions and undertake initiatives themselves. The Bureau has created a platform for Fanling's open class innovation to flourish in its own school and throughout its wider network.

SUMMARY

Lesson study or learning study in the form of open class is a deliberate design of collaborative professionalism to bring about improvement and change. It involves rigorous cycles of collaborative planning, review, practice, feedback, and public presentation in an environment that means the lesson belongs to everyone and that the problems, like the successes, are attributable to no one individual specifically. It is a design that shields professional learning and failure from the possibility of personal shame and blame.

Open class prospers because of the ingenuity and integration of its design elements that deepen the dialogue and welcome critical feedback about teaching and learning in the environment of real practice. At the same time, while the tools and protocols of open class have deepened preexisting and more informal processes of collaboration, they have not initiated effective collaboration where it did not exist before. They are supported and sustained by a surrounding professional culture where other kinds of collaboration prevail as an ethic of working and improvement. Open class and its teachers also benefit from a culture that is eager to learn and open to learning from elsewhere

> Precise methods of professionally coordinated collaboration occur within cultures and traditions that value the collective good, individual sacrifice, harmony, hierarchy, and humility.

in Hong Kong, on the Chinese mainland, and overseas. And it is enabled, though not micromanaged, by a policy system that encourages, expects, and actively supports pedagogical innovation and collaborative professional development. Not least, in high-performing Asian systems similar to those in Hong Kong, Singapore, and Japan, precise methods of professionally coordinated collaboration occur within cultures and traditions that value the collective good, individual sacrifice, harmony, hierarchy, and humility in a context that accords high value to and respect for learning, teaching, expertise, and authority.

NOTES

1. DuFour, R., & Eaker, R. (1998). *Professional learning communities at work: Best practices for enhancing student achievement.* Alexandria, VA: Association for Supervision and Curriculum Development; Lortie, D. (1975). *Schoolteacher.* Chicago, IL: University of Chicago Press.
2. Rosenholtz, S. J. (1989). *Teacher's workplace: The social organization of schools.* New York, NY: Longman.
3. Hattie, J. (2012). *Visible learning for teachers: Maximizing impact on learning.* Oxford, UK: Routledge.
4. All following quotations come from interviews and observations at Fanling school during a February 2017 research visit, unless otherwise stated.
5. Zimmerman, B. J., & Schunk, D. H. (Eds.). (2001). *Self-regulated learning and academic achievement: Theoretical perspectives.* Oxford, UK: Routledge.
6. Note from the school's open class PowerPoint presentation.
7. Stigler, J., & Hiebert, J. (1999). *The teaching gap.* New York, NY: Free Press.
8. Ibid.
9. Akita, K., & Sakamoto, A. (2015). Lesson study and teachers' professional development in Japan. In K. Wood & S. Sithamparam (Eds.), *Realising learning: Teachers' professional development through lesson and learning study* (pp. 25–40). London, UK: Sage; Arani, M. R. S., Fukaya, K., & Lassegard, J. P. (2010). "Lesson study" as professional culture in Japanese schools: An historical perspective on elementary classroom practices. *Nichibunken Japan Review,* 171–200; Perry, R. R., & Lewis, C. C. (2009). What is successful adaptation of lesson study in the U.S.? *Journal of Educational Change, 10*(4), 365–391.

10. Lewis, C., & Takahashi, A. (2013). Facilitating curriculum reforms through lesson study. *International Journal for Lesson and Learning Studies*, *2*(3), 207–217; World Association of Lesson Studies. (n.d.). *About WALS*. Retrieved from http://www.walsnet.org/about-wals.html

11. Cheng, E. C., & Lo, M. L. (2013). Learning study: Its origins, operationalisation, and implications (OECD Education Working Papers, No. 94). Paris, France: OECD. http://dx.doi.org/10.1787/5k3wjp0s959p-en

12. Marton, F. (2009). *Sameness and difference in learning.* Lecture at the Swedish Research Links Symposium on Phenomenography and Variation Theory, University of Hong Kong, Hong Kong SAR, December 1–3.

13. Lo, M.–L. (2009). The development of the learning study approach in classroom research in Hong Kong. *Educational Research Journal*, *24*(1), 165–184.

14. Elliott, J. (2016). Significant themes in developing the theory and practice of lesson study. *International Journal for Lesson and Learning Studies*, *5*(4), 274–280.

15. Lewis, C. (2000, April). *Lesson study: The core of Japanese professional development.* Paper presented at the American Educational Research Association Meeting, New Orleans, LA.

16. Lewis, C. (2002). Does lesson study have a future in the United States? *Nagoya Journal of Education and Human Development*, *1*, 1–23.

17. Datnow, A., & Park, V. (2014). *Data-driven leadership.* New York, NY: Jossey-Bass; Wohlstetter, P., Datnow, A., & Park, V. (2008). Creating a system for data-driven decision-making: Applying the principal-agent framework. *School Effectiveness and School Improvement*, *19*(3), 239–259.

18. Liu, P. (2016). A framework for understanding Chinese leadership: A cultural approach. *International Journal of Leadership in Education*, 1–13.

19. Sato, N. E. (2004). *Inside Japanese classrooms: The heart of education.* New York, NY: Routledge Falmer.

20. Kim-Eng Lee, C., & Mun Ling, L. (2013). The role of lesson study in facilitating curriculum reforms. *International Journal for Lesson and Learning Studies*, *2*(3), 200–206.

21. So, K., & Kim, J. (2013). Informal inquiry for professional development among teachers within a self-organized learning community: A case study from South Korea. *International Education Studies*, *6*(3), 105–115.

22. National Center for Education and the Economy. (n.d.). *Hong Kong overview.* Retrieved from http://ncee.org/what-we-do/center-on-international-education-benchmarking/top-performing-countries/hong-kong-overview/

23. This includes a team that was trained by one of us in an administrator development program in Toronto in 2000.

24. National Center for Education and the Economy. (n.d.). *Hong Kong overview*. Retrieved from http://ncee.org/what-we-do/center-on-international-education-benchmarking/top-performing-countries/hong-kong-overview/

25. KK Chan, interview, February 2017.

26. OECD. (2014). *Measuring innovation in education: A new perspective.* Paris, France: Author. http://dx.doi.org/10.1787/9789264215696-en

27. OECD. (2017). *PISA 2015 results (Volume III): Students' well-being.* Paris, France: Author. http://dx.doi.org/10.1787/9789264273856-en

CHAPTER
4

Collaborative Curriculum Planning Networks

COLLABORATION IN RURAL ENVIRONMENTS

"We all live in the sticks."[1] These are the words of Martha, a high school teacher of English Language Arts (ELA) in a rural school in Washington State, in the United States, about the network of rural school educators to which she belongs. Schools similar to Martha's find it hard to get access to what can come so easily to teachers in towns and cities: other colleagues who teach your own grade level, who share the same curriculum, or who can come down the corridor to give some ideas, advice, or moral support if you're having a rough day. But "in the sticks," teachers often find that they have to do pretty much everything themselves.

Martha's school is so small, she is the only teacher of her subject. So, she cannot repeat a lesson she has prepared for different classes. "When you're teaching four or five or six preps a day each year, and they can change from year to year, you don't have that luxury of time" to collaborate with other teachers, she says. In small, rural high schools, you are so busy teaching, you hardly have time to plan. And, in Martha's words, if you're the only teacher of your subject, "it's hard to collaborate with yourself!"

This is the double disadvantage of education in rural America. In former manufacturing towns where the industries have closed down, among poor immigrant agricultural workers, on Native American reservations, or in forestry communities that have been all logged out, working people struggle as much as they do in bigger cities. But they are also isolated from large centers of commerce, higher education, philanthropy, and investment. And they are often isolated from each other, too.

Although Martha and her colleagues in the vast region of the Pacific Northwest are often surrounded by spectacular natural beauty, they also work with communities who are faced with many kinds of deprivation. This includes their own professional isolation. So, teachers and principals from 27 of these districts, including Martha, have started to do something about the isolation. If they can conquer this, they believe, they will be better equipped to combat the problems posed by rural deprivation for the students they teach.

Twice a year, Martha and her colleagues drive over mountain passes and across state lines to get to places such as Spokane, Washington, where she and teachers and administrators from other rural schools and communities convene for 2 days as members of the Northwest Rural Innovation and Student Engagement (NW RISE) network. Some of them take multiple flights to come all the way from Alaska for these convenings. What brings them here, other than the additional attraction of bigger and better shopping?

At 7:30 a.m., the hotel ballroom is already filled with the lively chatter of friends and colleagues reuniting and catching up after many months apart. Like other professionals, teachers are notorious for wanting to talk shop. But these educators have come to Spokane for more than a bit of chit-chat. They have come to *work*. During their two-and-a-bit days in this small city, teachers from rural and remote schools in Alaska, Idaho, Oregon, and Washington will listen to presentations, share ideas, and fill out online surveys about their students' learning and their school's progress in real time. Most of all and most of the time, though, educators will get together in what their own survey responses have indicated are their most valuable groups. These are job-alike groups of colleagues working with similar subjects or groups of students across their schools, such as math teachers, kindergarten teachers, teachers of special needs, and school administrators. In their own schools, sometimes hours from the next school, rural educators are often the only teachers of their grade or their subject. They have no one else in similar situations to connect with or learn from. This is why Martha really values her own job-alike group of English language teachers.

JOB-ALIKE COLLABORATION

Like educators in the other job-alike groups, Martha's group is trying to plan lessons, experiences, and units of work with her colleagues that will increase their students' engagement with their learning and with their life within and beyond their community (Figure 4.1). David,[2] a younger ELA teacher from rural Oregon, appreciates this work on lesson planning, especially when resources may be few and far between. "As a new teacher, it's overwhelming to plan so many different activities," David says. When you live in an isolated area and don't have other teachers to talk to about your ideas, "just the fact that some people can get around a table and help to plan activities can be so beneficial and helpful."

"The challenge is, you sometimes feel like you're on an island," another NW RISE teacher says. "I'm the only fifth-grade teacher, and there's times when I think, where am I going to go for ideas?"[3] All staff members are pulled in many different directions with multiple responsibilities, including the principal. "I'm the superintendent, principal, bus driver, custodian, part time, all of those,"[4] one

says. But, he continues, NW RISE has offered something new that is helping him and his school rethink teaching and learning:

> *Joining NW RISE was a great opportunity for us to link us with other small, rural schools. For the first time in my principalship, I felt like here's a group of people that really get the challenges that I have.*[5]

FOCUS ON ENGAGEMENT

Student engagement is the focus of the NW RISE network—and for a good reason. Globally, the number of students in rural areas who do not have access to education and who are not in schools is twice as large—16% compared to 8%—as in urban communities.[6] In the United States, over 40% of K–12 schools are located in rural communities. Almost one third of all U.S. students attend rural schools.[7] Eighty-five percent of the persistently poor counties in the United States (ones in which 20% of the population has lived below the poverty line for the last 30 years or more) are classified as *rural counties*.[8] Other challenges of rural American communities include weak economic development, chronic absenteeism, low educational aspirations, poor achievement, and low high school and college completion rates.[9] In the Northwest United States, "66 percent of Northwest districts are in rural areas" and "nearly 500 rural schools in the [U.S.] Northwest have five or fewer teachers."[10]

In the United States and elsewhere, student achievement is closely connected to student engagement. Of course, it is possible to be resilient and to achieve without much immediate engagement—through perseverance, sacrifice, and grit. But if students' surrounding life circumstances are not supportive, then getting their attention above and beyond all the other things they have to cope with—living in poverty, going hungry, looking after younger siblings, or encountering drugs or violence in the family or community—is usually a prerequisite for success.[11] For teachers in the NW RISE network, this means learning to work with and plan around what students and their rural communities have as well as what they lack. And it means working with other rural teachers (and their students) to create the inspiration, ideas, curriculum, and assessments that can bring their students' learning alive.

Some of the value of these collaborative planning teams is simply about realizing that, different as these teachers' circumstances are, they

> Doing something deliberately to try to make a difference together is what deeper collaborative professionalism is about.

are ultimately all in the same boat. "These teachers are down in the trenches fighting to keep kids from dropping out, from committing suicide, and from getting pregnant," says one of Martha's fellow collaborators. "And we're one-on-one with these kids. It gets to you. . . . And so, this has given us a chance to see that there are others just like us. . . . It's very rewarding."

There's more to deep professional collaboration than the ability to relate or commiserate, though. Misery may love company sometimes, but it doesn't get people out of bed and off to school or work. Doing something deliberately to try to make a difference together is what deeper collaborative professionalism is about.

THE ELA JOB-ALIKE GROUP

Chris Spriggs described how she, Martha, and another founding member of the ELA job-alike group got started: "We had decided that we really, truly wanted to focus on student engagement, but that we wanted to focus on authentic learning." Danette Parsley, chief program officer at Education Northwest and the instigator of the NW RISE network, speaking in support of the ELA group, said,

> This is not an academic exercise. This is real work—and really relevant, in real time. They don't treat this as something separate, or something in addition to what they're doing. This is adding value to what they need to do tomorrow, the next day, the next month. And they use each other as supports to do their work. . . . The ELA group was right out on the front line as a model.

As their first project together, Chris and the other group members picked the task of teaching their ninth- to eleventh-grade students how to write and defend an argument. In a world of wild opinions where too many people think they are experts[12] and where arguments are reduced to shouting matches even on national TV, these teachers understood that making a defensible argument is not only a college requirement; it is an essential tool of democratic reason.

In the first year, the ELA group's argument topic asked students to adopt a stance toward 1:1 technology implementation in their schools and write an argument with reasons and evidence to convince a designated audience of their position (including anticipating any objections to the argument). Different community-based audiences for these arguments included school, district, or community members with whom the students interacted and to whom they directed their writing. With a touch of authenticity, these groups included the district technology board and a potential community funder.

The argument topic in the next year had students adopt a stance on the use of drones, which could include private, public, or government use, depending on the particular project and audience. Other ELA projects have involved day-in-the-life time-lapse videos in which students use smartphones to film and describe their local, rural communities to one another in ways that build pride in their own communities alongside understanding of others' communities. All of these projects enhance writing by increasing engagement. Students learn about different genres and structures of writing and about how to consider different writing purposes and audiences in authentic practices that enable them to share their own life experience, reflect on their identity, and interact with other rural community members. But most importantly, many of the projects (including writing arguments) have involved connecting the students so that they can collaborate to work on their writing. As Chris explained, the teachers "put the kids together, and then they are given a common peer-editing rubric that they use to give feedback and post onto Schoology [a digital platform] for their peers to read."

What impact has this work had on students? Chris noticed how "the students talk a lot more about these other schools. They reference kids, they talk about how they want to go there [to the other schools] and visit, they want to do more, they want to participate more." In addition, she said,

> They've learned a lot more about the actual writing process because I don't think I would have spent as much diligent, meticulous time breaking down each part of the writing process as I do now with the group. I think it's made the students more alert to audience when they're writing. It's made them pay way more attention to their word choice.

Students agreed. One of them who had written about drones to their rural community's state representative said,

> I took the project a lot more seriously. I thought I could be heard. So I tried to express how I felt about drones and tried to get my

point across clearly. I was just trying to sound more professional. I wasn't trying to use slang or anything like that. I was trying to use words that would get my point across. Because I felt like the state representative, if he was just to read it and it was just me talking like how I would with my friends, he wouldn't take me seriously and [would] just push my paper aside.

Students advanced many arguments. One discussed the value of drones for surveying her agricultural and farming community. Others worried about invasions of privacy. By engaging in peer feedback across schools, they were able to improve each other's writing while also considering these different perspectives.

Of course, having high school students collaborate via technology can also pose risks, such as students posting inappropriate remarks to their peers in other schools. As Chris explained, though, students "had to learn about 'netiquette' and speaking to one another properly online and not using Schoology like a social media site." These kinds of lessons (including writing apologies to recipients of inappropriate remarks!) helped students to learn and develop as people, to provide feedback to improve writing, and to empathize with "people who live in a much different world than you do."

Danette Parsley described how the work of the ELA group has inspired other job-alike groups:

Engaging students—that was an unexpected thing that took off from the ELA group. They were really early adopters. That group used the collaboration protocols. They got to know each other, landed on a project, and said argument writing is something we all need to do. It developed into a combination of sharing resources, designing some lessons, and not too far into it, they realized, "Wait a minute, instead of us just designing lessons together, why not get our kids involved?" They were on the front edge, which I think is brilliant. Now I see this trickling over to some of the other job-alikes, and it's so energizing.

The network's success not only hinges on the network coordinators. It also comes from teachers taking leadership roles, making their collaborative projects meaningful, and encouraging one another in their work. Much went into the design of the NW RISE network to enable it to be this way.

NETWORK DESIGN

Like some of the best educational networks before and alongside it, NW RISE has a specific and deliberate design.[13] Not all networks, including educational networks, are designed in the same way, though. They have different content or purposes, such as disseminating innovation,[14] supporting improvement, or implementing change.[15]

Networks can also assume different forms. Mark Hadfield and Chris Chapman[16] outline three different kinds of networks.

- *Hub-and-spoke networks* are organized around a central hub where information is disseminated to participants on the periphery.

- *Nodal systems* comprise mini-hubs; schools are clustered together by region, level, or focus to implement and give feedback on government policies and strategies.

- *Crystalline networks* have no recognizable hubs. Interactions occur across the network on multiple and overlapping pathways of communication.[17]

NETWORK PRINCIPLES

The design team determined eight elements that were characteristic of successful, high-performing networks and used these to inform the design of NW RISE.[18]

1. **Shared Goals**: *Shared goals are determined early and are relevant, purposeful, and desirable for all network members.* After much discussion, the NW RISE design team decided that their focus would be on increasing students' engagement with their learning and their communities by building the

professional capital and especially the social capital of teachers across rural communities so they could collaborate more effectively.[19,20] These strategies, it was determined, should also fit statewide and federal concerns of getting students college and career ready and should not add to teachers' and administrators' workloads.

2. **Site Selection and Participation**: *Potential members view participation as being attractive and worth the effort.* The first core group of schools—only nine to begin with—were approached by state leaders on the grounds of being ready and willing to participate in terms of their own local needs. Additionally, the design team determined that the network would be for "small" districts, approximately 400 or fewer students in one K–12 campus, to create a network of similar districts and schools.

3. **Form of Networking Activities**: *This depends on the size and purpose of the network, but the more that activities involve teachers themselves, the more likely that collective responsibility will be established.* Once the initial group of schools met, the first task (in addition to building relationships) was for each job-alike group to choose its focus. Some, like the ELA group, found this quickly; one found it perhaps too quickly and then had to step back and regroup (a problem that Michael Fullan calls *false clarity*[21]); and some had to go well beyond the first convening to figure out what they could work on together. In the end, though, each group determined its direction for itself and did not have a purpose imposed on it.

4. **Focus**: *Network members must decide what activities will be most useful to achieve the network goals.* Job-alike groups became an early favorite of network members and remained the major point of focus throughout. Technology-based communication evolved more slowly. Inputs by Education Northwest and Boston College productively disturbed existing mindsets, as did invited presentations from outside experts. Open space technology, where participants could offer their own presentations in a fair format, led to sessions being presented on a wide range of topics.

5. **Steering**: *High-quality leadership supports, directs, and facilitates, but also allows space for distributed leadership.* The design and mix of activities and engagements was carefully designed by the steering committee and informed by continuous participant feedback. For instance, the Education Northwest team provided a collaboration and implementation protocol—SPUR—that was used to guide the collaboration process in a purposeful way through a process of brainstorming, reflection, planning, implementation, and then more reflection.[22]

6. **Resources**: *Leaders can help to provide resources, but they should also empower other network members to become proactive about commitment and securing support.* The federal grant that Education Northwest successfully secured made the network possible in the first place, but long before the midpoint and after a presentation by us on principles of sustainability,[23] network members and state representatives discussed how to access and, indeed, donate their own resources to make the network sustainable beyond the term of the grant. Green, yellow, and red paddles were raised during steering committee meetings to signify agreement or the need for additional discussion on these crucial points.

7. **Network Citizenship**: *There need to be clear rules about participation.* These norms and rules were especially important to job-alike groups who had to agree how and how much to communicate digitally between convenings and to present webinars to other members on topics of their choosing.

8. **Spread and Growth**: *New participants, purposes, and activities will emerge, and both growth and change will have to be acknowledged and dealt with.* The network members continue to discuss, decide, reflect on, and review how much and how fast they should grow in order to have greater reach versus how they can maintain the intimacy of the smaller group interaction that enabled them to build trust and mutual understanding. This is one of several common dilemmas of networks discussed by Lieberman and Grolnick.[24] At present, after four years of planning (three of which have comprised in-person school convenings), the network has tripled in size.

NETWORK TECHNOLOGY

The benefits and drawbacks of technology for innovative professional development are hotly debated. Whatever the merits of the overall arguments on either side, in rural communities (assuming there is broadband capability), digital technology makes shared professional learning available in ways that could not be offered in any other form.

The platform used by the ELA job-alike group as well as all NW RISE network members is Schoology, a learning management system that provides a virtual digital space to share resources, to post comments and engage in dialogue asynchronously, and to conduct collaborative meetings in real time. Having both asynchronous and real-time options to collaborate means that teachers can work across time zones and within different school schedules while also setting aside intentional time to virtually meet "face-to-face." Though the teachers use e-mail, Google Docs and other Google platforms, and Skype to connect and collaborate, having a central platform such as Schoology for all project resources and a reliable virtual meeting system has helped the group to stay organized and map out their future plans.

Together, the in-person meetings and digital and virtual connections create a balanced and blended approach to collaboration. The in-person convenings provide the foundations for relationships, trust, and substantive lesson planning. The technology, meanwhile, allows for the implementation of projects, regular check-ins between in-person meetings, and the ability to engage students more directly in the work. This progression from teacher to student collaboration made the collaborative work especially relevant and impactful for teachers and students alike.

> In rural communities (assuming there is broadband capability), digital technology makes shared professional learning available in ways that could not be offered in any other form.

SUMMARY

"We believe that teachers working with teachers is the most effective way that you can improve schools," says Danette Parsley. "We believe that teachers are professionals who have way more to offer to each other than perhaps they're ever given the opportunity to ever elevate and express, especially in small, rural schools." For Danette, professional collaboration doesn't merely amount to setting teachers free, though. She and Education Northwest "wanted to provide scaffolding for job-alike groups." However, "once the flame hits, you don't need to provide the scaffolding anymore." Chris Spriggs, for example, is now facilitator of the ELA group as she encourages other teacher leaders to reflect upon their students' needs to drive new collaborative projects. From the argument-writing project to the day-in-the-life student films about community and identity, these planning ideas were driven by the teachers, who in turn were inspired by their students, rather than being directed by their principals.

In the NW RISE network, teachers work with teachers and schools work with schools in relation to authentic purposes and audiences and with the engagement of their students. This benefits the students and also retains the commitment and ignites the fire in teachers. Chris talks about the impact of the network on herself and other rural teachers:

> They get rejuvenated, excited; they go back, they talk to the other teachers about it. And for me, it's completely changed my thinking. I've been so isolated as a teacher. I just have gotten used to being my own boss and doing what I want and making my decisions. And then I have to come here and hear ideas that don't necessarily go with mine and learn to be flexible and see others' perspectives. It's also been nice just to work with other people who have the same frustrations. They don't get paid very much, but they do 20 jobs and work late nights and they coach and they advise. That's just been something that's been enlightening and helped me. But it really has changed my life to come here and work and be around everyone.

Another teacher says the network has "reinvigorated my teaching style. I try new things. I work with these teachers and have collaborated a lot more." A secondary history teacher echoes these words:

> *What I love about the [network], it's the only one that I know that is totally focused on rural schools. So many of these conferences, I'm [typically] the odd man out because I have a class of eight kids. The other teachers have no idea what that's like. Whereas when I go to an NW RISE conference or jump on Schoology, I know everyone's on the same page.*[25]

NW RISE network members aren't all on the same page by coincidence. A carefully and intentionally designed network architecture, along with creating space for teachers to be agents of their own improvement, led to a form of collaboration that is both deep and sustainable in an unlikely place—the rural and often remote U.S. Pacific Northwest.

NOTES

1. All ensuing quotations come from interviews and observations at an NW RISE network meeting during a December 2016 research visit, unless otherwise stated.
2. A pseudonym.
3. Education Northwest. (2016, January 19). *NW RISE: Connecting rural schools*. Retrieved from https://www.youtube.com/watch?v=UYRu_-Ag0xY
4. Ibid.
5. Ibid.
6. Beckman, P. J., & Gallo, J. (2016). Rural education in a global context. *Global Education Review*, *2*(4), 1–4. Retrieved from http://ger.mercy.edu/index.php/ger/article/viewFile/238/15; UNESCO. (2015). *EFA global monitoring report: Education for all 2000–2015 achievements and challenges*. Paris, France: Author.
7. Battelle for Kids. (2016). *Generating opportunity and prosperity: The promise of rural educational collaboratives*. Retrieved from http://battelleforkids.org/docs/default-source/publications/generatingopportunityprosperityview.pdf?sfvrsn=2
8. Ibid.; Cohen, R. (2014, December 4). What ails rural philanthropy, and what must be done. *Nonprofit Quarterly*. Retrieved from http://

nonprofitquarterly.org/2014/12/04/what-ails-rural-communities-philanthropy-what-must-be-done/

9. Budge, K. (2006). Rural leaders, rural places: Problem, privilege, and possibility. *Journal of Research in Rural Education, 21*(13), 1–10; Irvin, M. J., Byun, S., Meece, J. L., Farmer, T. W., & Hutchins, B. C. (2012). Educational barriers of rural youth: Relation of individual and contextual difference variables. *Journal of Career Assessment, 20*(1), 71–87.

10. Education Northwest. (2016, January 19). *NW RISE: Connecting rural schools* [Video file]. Retrieved from https://www.youtube.com/watch?v=UYRu_-Ag0xY

11. Boykin, A. W., & Noguera, P. (2011). *Creating the opportunity to learn: Moving from research to practice to close the achievement gap.* Alexandria, VA: ASCD; Lawson, M. A., & Lawson, H. A. (2013). New conceptual frameworks for student engagement research, policy, and practice. *Review of Educational Research, 83*(3), 432–479.

12. Nichols, T. (2017). *The death of expertise: The campaign against established knowledge and why it matters.* New York, NY: Oxford University Press.

13. Daly, A. J. (2010). Mapping the terrain: Social network theory and educational change. In A. J. Daly (Ed.), *Social network theory and educational change* (pp. 1–16). Cambridge, MA: Harvard Education Press; Lieberman, A., Campbell, C., & Yashkina, A. (2016). *Teacher learning and leadership: Of, by, and for teachers (Teacher quality and school development).* Florence, KY: Taylor and Francis; Lieberman, A., & Grolnick, M. (1996). Networks and reform in American education. *Teachers College Record, 98*(1), 7–45.

14. Davis, B., Sumara, D., & D'Amour, L. (2012). Understanding school districts as learning systems: Some lessons from three cases of complex transformation. *Journal of Educational Change, 13*(3), 373–399.

15. Wellman, B., & Berkowitz, S. D. (Eds.). (1988). *Social structures: A network approach.* New York, NY: Cambridge University Press.

16. Hadfield, M., & Chapman, C. (2009). *Leading school-based networks.* London, UK: Routledge.

17. See Hargreaves, A., Parsley, D., & Cox, E. K. (2015). Designing rural school improvement networks: Aspirations and actualities. *Peabody Journal of Education, 90*(2), 306–321.

18. Ibid.

19. Hargreaves, A., & Fullan, M. (2012). *Professional capital: Transforming teaching in every school.* New York, NY: Teachers College Press.

20. Leana, C. R. (2011, Fall). The missing link in school reform. *Stanford Social Innovation Review*, 30–35.

21. Fullan, M., & Stiegelbauer, S. (1991). *The new meaning of educational change* (2nd ed.). Toronto, Ontario, Canada: Ontario Institute for Studies in Education.

22. *SPUR* stands for *set the focus, plan for change, undertake change,* and *recharge and sustain.*

23. Hargreaves, A., & Fink, D. (2006). *Sustainable leadership.* San Francisco, CA: Jossey-Bass.

24. Lieberman, A., & Grolnick, M. (1996). Networks and reform in American education. *Teachers College Record, 98*(1), 7–45.

25. Education Northwest. (2016, January 19). *NW RISE: Connecting rural schools* [Video file]. Retrieved from https://www.youtube.com/watch?v=UYRu_-Ag0xY

CHAPTER

5

Cooperative Learning and Working

There are strong cases for increasing collaborative professionalism in many educational systems. But what is the argument for investing further in teachers' professional capital and especially social capital in countries that are already affluent and where traditions of democratic decision making have become integral features of the society? One of the wealthiest countries per capita on the planet is Norway.[1] It tops the United Nations Human Development index and its people were rated the happiest in the world in 2017.[2]

Collaboration may not be new to Norwegian society, but it is relatively new for Norwegian teachers. Outside its three or four cities, in a nation of only four million people, Norway has historically been a rural society in which teachers spent much of their time working in small schools. This gave them a lot of individual authority and autonomy in their own schools and classes. Many teachers also had other jobs, such as farming and running local stores, which left little time for collaboration outside their classrooms. This is one reason why teachers' time, even today, is calculated very precisely in their work contracts. What do the push and pull of these different factors and forces mean for how teachers collaborate in this society?

CONSISTENCY OF COOPERATION

Aronsloekka primary school, one of 19 schools in the municipality of Drammen, 45 kilometers southwest of Oslo, has been developing its own form of teacher collaboration over several years. The idea underpinning professional collaboration is to base the principles for interaction and learning among teachers on the principles of learning and interaction among students. The school has invested heavily in cooperative learning and believes that there should be consistency in the forms of cooperation within classes and among teachers.

We have seen cooperative learning in action ever since one of us worked with Michael Fullan in Ontario, Canada, in the late 1980s to build a consortium of four school boards that based much of their initial work around training in cooperative learning and classroom management. Early evaluations indicated that the training processes were highly successful, but that after initial summer institutes for teachers, many schools did not follow through because of weak support from the principal or the wider culture of the school. Many teachers weren't able to persist in getting their children to cooperate unless there was a culture where the teachers cooperated, too. This is why consistency between student and teacher cooperation is essential.

Principal (in Norway, the term is *Rektor*) Lena Kilen and her deputy, Marcus Kathrud, understand this very well. In our site visit at the end of May in 2017, we observed cooperative learning in classrooms and also as an organizing principle for teacher meetings.[3] The method of cooperative learning used in Aronsloekka was based on the work of U.S. expert Spencer Kagan, which provides up to 250 classroom strategies to improve academic achievement and develop students' social skills and team building.[4] When we walked into one of the primary classes, cooperative learning strategies were clearly evident. Children had to talk about the goal of the Norwegian language lesson. They stood and "mixed up" by snaking around the room as in a game of musical chairs, and then they found partners for a brief, reciprocal discussion. They started by talking about how they would cooperate, how they would discuss together, right down to the pitch of their voice. They stood and mixed up once more with different partners to discuss three difficult Norwegian words that have a *kj* sound.

There is meta-cognition at work here—children were thinking about how they work together. Five of the most popular Kagan strategies were listed on the board. Three of them were being used on this day. One of the most widely adopted, here and elsewhere, is *round robin*, in which children take turns to respond orally in their group. Another is *rally coach*, in which one partner coaches the other in solving a problem, then they exchange roles. In doing so, they explain aloud what they are thinking. These strategies are good for "listening, showing respect, and helping," says Lena. The teachers use the standard strategies from the Kagan playbook, but also invent their own if student needs require it. As the class proceeds, it is clear that the children are very familiar with the strategies, and like their peers in Fanling in Hong Kong, they know what to do.

One of the teachers explains aspects of the group formation. Groups are mixed ability—again, like Fanling—with the highest and lowest in a group of four being "face partners" and those in between being "shoulder partners" "so they can help each other if one gets stuck." This "stops the mind [from] wandering" so that "more [of them] finish on time when they do [the work] together."

At the end of the morning, a school staff meeting exhibits many of the same principles and processes that are evident in the cooperative learning classroom. The meeting engages staff in determining the goals for the school and connecting these to the long-term, 5-year (2016–2020) quality plan that the school compiles to share with the municipality.[5]

There is ice cream and relaxed social conversation at the start of the meeting. A repeat of the earlier class structure is evident as teachers snake around each other once more, form pairs, and then, for 30 seconds each, using the Kagan methods that the principal names in the meeting, they discuss what inspiration and motivation are. Now the task is to return to their corners in groups the principal has carefully composed and discuss how to get students from being inspired to being motivated. The reason for this is to think about how a data-informed focus can result in teachers thinking about many students who are merely in the middle rather than high up in the range of achievement results. In one of the groups, teachers talk about needing to pair up with someone to learn more about the cooperative learning structures. Another shared her wish to double the number of methods in her repertoire.

For a while, Lena takes over and connects discussion to data in the quality plan, indicating that 56% of their students report that they look forward to going to school. This is better than the municipality average, she points out, but she emphasizes that this is still bad for many children. They have a "moral purpose that they owed the students something," she insists. Their motivation, perseverance, and experiences of dealing with failure have to be addressed. This means using the Kagan structures more extensively and more deeply, the teachers conclude. They must try to move from levels three to four of Kagan implementation.

Finally, back in their groups, teachers work quietly on reviewing and revising statements they had drafted in relation to their school goals the previous week. The conversation is quiet and restrained—quite different from Hong Kong! This exercise is not simply a matter of technical drafting. Teachers raise examples that challenge their thinking, such as how to reconcile the mother who was concerned that her child was introverted and didn't want to be in groups all the time against the importance of helping children to become more social and ensuring that "it is not so easy for kids to hide anymore."

> All teachers can see what they are part of, how they contribute, and where their responsibilities lie.

Lena and Marcus "want teachers also to be leaders

and big picture thinkers." The teachers work together on a range of things in teams. Like other schools with professional learning communities (PLCs), for example, some teams focus on specific topics where teachers share strategies in relation to reading, social skills, math, and cooperative learning itself. Everyone has the opportunity to be in one of these groups, Lena explains. But in addition, teachers are also involved in "how they run the school; on developing the school and its directions. . . . They plan the next meetings as they know what the next step is." This includes deciding what the priorities will be and what kind of culture they will have. "There is no way you fall asleep in our staff meetings," Lena says.

In many schools around the world, teacher collaboration or PLCs translate into working on specific aspects of pedagogy or the curriculum that have immediate or short-term impact on teachers' own classrooms. The big picture is left to the principal and the senior management. But at Aronsloekka, as we will also see in the Colombian schools of *Escuela Nueva* in the next chapter, all teachers can see what they are part of, how they contribute, and where their responsibilities lie.

CONTEXT OF COOPERATION

Where has the idea of organizing staff teams to resemble cooperative learning lessons with children come from? What inspired it, drives it, and sustains it now? To address this question, we will turn to the points raised in our discussion of open class and lesson study. What went *before*? What other collaborative processes occur *betwixt* the cooperative learning? How does the policy system in the municipality and the country stand, on the shoulder, *beside* the cooperative learning design? And how do the teachers and principals find inspiration, training, stimulation, and connection *beyond* the school?

1. Before

The previous principal, as one experienced member of staff recalled, had created an environment where teachers felt secure, but she controlled much of the detail of decision making. She decided "where the cupboards were, the color of the curtains, the selection of the books." So, the teachers were "not used to professional decisions."

When Lena arrived 5 years ago, teachers had collaborated, she noticed. They would "tell each other what they have been doing, talk together, see what others were doing." But this didn't run very deep. Indeed, sometimes the collaboration resulted in the gossip and storytelling of Judith Warren Little's characterization of weak collaboration.[6] "Talking about each other was one of the dinosaurs that would be left behind." "If we don't agree, it is better to say it when we are together. Building a positive culture is so hard," Lena continued. "When the days are good and bright, it is easy. But when they are gray, it is not." Lena emphasizes that "if you don't participate, you cannot complain after." And in meetings, if "teachers talk about other things," the principal and deputy stand beside them so that "they feel uncomfortable eventually."

Before the coexistence of cooperative learning in teacher culture as well as students' classrooms, there also had to be prior investment in the cooperative learning itself. Teachers were sent on intensive training courses to Manchester, England, until a critical mass of them built up in the school. But not all the early efforts were successful. One teacher explained that when they started, "Kagan didn't work." Children were "shoving each other, [and] crawling on the floor, [they] wouldn't do as they were told." The teacher had to spend 6 months to establish a safe learning environment. She moved away from Kagan for a while to reestablish basic behaviors such as having children raise their hand. "Kagan has no theory of having an orderly environment in place," the teacher commented. Only once order was reestablished was cooperative learning reintroduced.

Different teachers progressed at different speeds, but they all worked together in supporting each other in moving forward. Failure, and stepping back sometimes, had to be experienced and undertaken before achieving the more consistent success that is evident today. The method is not successful all by itself. It is influenced and sometimes enabled by all the work that goes before and around it.

2. Betwixt

In the classroom and the staffroom alike, cooperative learning at Aronsloekka does not exist as the only collaborative initiative, as an island in space and time. It is, of course, a specific methodology (of U.S. origin) acquired via trainers or institutes in the United Kingdom. But similar to other initiatives, it matters how externally appropriated methods and designs fit with and develop alongside the rest of the school culture.

First, there is the importance of nature and the outdoors as a place of learning and development. At recess, we walked around the schoolyard where children were playing. There was a friendship bench for students who have no one to play with (Figure 5.1). A soccer ball bounced down a ditch and across a small stream; a child went to collect it. There were no fences around the playground.

Like in other Scandinavian countries, schools embrace the outdoors. Whole-school assemblies addressed by the principal are held outside, even in the middle of winter. In Norway, they say, there is no such thing as bad weather. There is only bad gear. At Christmas, children and their teachers go into the woods together. In autumn, they pick blueberries. In summer, they play in the river and make campfires. Play, nature, and conversation are seen as ways of building relationships and creating memories together—children and adults all together, for this is where adults and children alike, every day, see parts of each other that are not always visible in the classroom. School, say Lena and Marcus, teaches children "to love how to move, to get around and be with your friends, [and] to learn to talk." Similar to an indigenous community in Northwest Ontario and rural schools in the jungles of Colombia that will be introduced in subsequent chapters, schools work *with* the environment, not *against* it.

Norwegian education also emphasizes the importance of the whole child and his or her development. Cooperation is part of this. One of the four pillars of the official Norwegian curriculum is to communicate, collaborate, and participate. Another is to explore, inquire, and create. One of the reasons we have schools, Lena says,

Figure 5.1 Two children on the school's friendship bench.

Source: Aronsloekka Primary School

is to "make people feel good about themselves; [to] be part of a community—to be good in subjects but also [in] being a person and being active."

Sixth graders teach computer coding to first graders. Teachers plan collaborative lessons using iPads and also Lego materials. They send pictures home digitally so parents can see that the school "is a good place for the child to be." This "builds relations with parents in peaceful situations" and makes it easier to address "difficult stuff" later on. Cooperative learning as a strategy or a particular design is therefore surrounded by many other ways of building collaboration among the children and all the adults connected with the school.

When Norwegian educators go to Manchester in the United Kingdom to participate in the Kagan training institutes, they also become aware of how their own system and culture are distinct. Teachers in England are formal, one teacher noted. They are addressed as *Sir* and *Miss*. The men wear shirts and ties. Teachers in Norway, however, are called by their first name. "Children have a different mindset in Norway," one of the teachers said. "They don't fear the teacher." This means thinking carefully about how the precise methodologies of cooperative learning are applied in the more informal setting of Norwegian schools.

3. Beside

The policy system in Norway also supports the collaborative direction in which Aronsloekka is moving. Norwegian curriculum goals are very broad and leave considerable space for school and teacher discretion. Time bargains between unions and government also enable collaborative efforts. The contract for primary school teachers' work is 42 hours per week, with 32 of those to be spent at school. Nineteen of those are taken up with instructional time. Of the remaining 13 hours a week, 9 are allocated for personal planning and assessing, with the remaining 4 being up to the principal's discretion—though she or he usually discusses how to use these with the union representatives.

One priority, especially since we met toward the end of the school year, is the annual plan and planning process for the municipality's quality review. In the past years, partly as a result of networks to and connections with the Ontario educational system, most municipalities have introduced data systems to monitor progress toward educational goals. The data are reviewed internally and also between the principal and the director of the municipality. "I have to know my numbers," Lena says. But, she feels, the use of data adds more precision to some of the school's discussions and decisions. There are some affirmations, such as the fact that Drammen's value-added improvement score is greater than anywhere else in Norway. There are also questions about the fact that girls are not achieving as well as boys in reading (which contradicts the national trend), the need for improvement with the growing number of children from immigrant families, and large numbers of children "in the middle," who are above proficiency but would benefit from greater challenge.

These issues are discussed with staff to support their planning processes, but they do not constitute separate data teams with special funding for specified problems that replace or override all the other kinds of professional collaboration that exist in the school. The use of data is part of a wider collaborative and improvement strategy, not the driving force or design of that strategy.

4. Beyond

Last, Aronsloekka has been able to adopt its own particular path by learning and networking from many other systems beyond it. It has learned a lot from connections to and visits with educators in Ontario and is part of a small network of schools that have formed a partnership between Alberta (Canada) and Norway. Also, of course, its adoption of the Kagan approach to cooperative learning derives from a U.S.-based approach that has been widely used in Canada and now provides training in the United Kingdom. The staff at Aronsloekka collaborate externally as well as internally.

SUMMARY

Happiness alone does not guarantee success. As the Aronsloekka school demonstrates, however, it is possible to marry a focus on the human dimensions of holistic education and development with school improvement lessons from around the world—from Kagan to Canada—to improve student outcomes. Lena, as school leader, has a deep awareness of the culture of her school and community and uses it as leverage. Additionally, she recognizes that together, teachers can do more when they are empowered to do so.

But most important, perhaps, is how collaboration can benefit both students and teachers—and how a holistic approach to collaboration can transform a school and the learning that happens within and beyond it.

NOTES

1. Treanor, S. (2014, August 27). How Norway has avoided the "curse of oil." *BBC News*. Retrieved from http://www.bbc.com/news/business-28882312
2. Helliwell, J., Layard, R., & Sachs, J. (2017). *World happiness report 2017*. New York, NY: Sustainable Development Solutions Network. Retrieved from http://worldhappiness.report/ed/2017/; United Nations Development Programme. (2016). *Human development reports: Norway*. Retrieved from http://hdr.undp.org/en/countries/profiles/NOR
3. Quotes from this point forward without unique endnotes are based on interviews from a research visit in June 2017.
4. Johnson, S., Marietta, G., Higgins, M. C., Mapp, K. L., & Grossman, A. (2015). *Achieving coherence in district improvement: Managing the relationship between the central office and schools*. Cambridge, MA: Harvard Education Press; Kagan, S. (1985). Dimensions of cooperative classroom structures. In R. Slavin, S. Sharan, S. Kagan, R. Hertz Lazarowitz, C. Webb, & R. Schmuck (Eds.), *Learning to cooperate, cooperating to learn*. New York, NY: Plenum; Kagan, S., & Kagan, M. (2015). *Kagan cooperative learning: Dr. Spencer Kagan and Miguel Hagan*. San Clemente, CA: Kagan; Li, M.P., & Lam, B. H. (2013). *Cooperative learning. The Hong Kong Institute of Education*. Retrieved from https://www.eduhk.hk/aclass/Theories/cooperativelearningcoursewriting_LBH%2024June.pdf; Slavin, R. (1999). Comprehensive approaches to cooperative learning. *Theory into Practice, 38*(2), 74–79.
5. Drammen Kommune. (2016). *Learning pathways Drammen: Succeeding all the way*. Drammen, Norway: Author.
6. Little, J. W. (1990). The persistence of privacy: Autonomy and initiative in teachers' professional relations. *Teachers College Record, 91*(4), 509–536.

CHAPTER
6

Collaborative Pedagogical Transformation

Aronsloekka is a case of collaborative professionalism that benefits from multiple partners working together in a well-resourced environment that enables international collaboration and training and is well supported in provisions of teacher time. Is this kind of collaborative professionalism a privilege and a prerogative of affluence? Is it unattainable in less-developed economies, especially where many teachers work in rural isolation?

In 1976, one woman, a teacher's daughter in Latin America, didn't believe so. At the age of 24, after returning home from completing two master's degrees at Stanford University, she set about transforming education in poor rural communities, then in cities, then in other parts of the world, to the point where her inspiring vision has been realized in over 25,000 schools.[1] Her name is Vicky Colbert. In 2013, Colbert was the first recipient of what was then the nearest thing to a Nobel Prize for education—the WISE Prize for Education—for successfully transforming learning for children in poor communities over almost 40 years in her native Colombia and also in 16 countries elsewhere. In 2017, she was then awarded the inaugural Yidan Prize of $4 million for her global contributions to educational development.

VISION OF *ESCUELA NUEVA*

However collaborative a movement may become, most social movements start off with an improbably inspiring vision or dream of one or two individuals.[2] Even in her mid-20s, Colbert knew that "if we don't have *quality* basic education, nothing will be achieved in any country in the world. You won't have social development, economic development, peace, democracy! It's the only way."[3] To give children in rural Colombia a chance, she and committed educators who came to work with her had to teach children the power of community, democracy, and engagement. Colbert and her colleagues, Óscar Mogollón and Beryl Levinger, didn't only want greater access to basic education or even to *quality* basic education in terms of providing more effective traditional teaching to improve performance in the basics. They wanted to transform learning in ways that gave it meaning and purpose for thousands and then millions of poor or disadvantaged children.

For Vicky Colbert, one of the founders of *Escuela Nueva (New School)*, the model has been her life's work, from starting out as a young idealist to becoming the "genial grandmother" she is today.[4] In a country that had been torn apart by violence, drugs, and corruption, she and her colleagues first began implementing and spreading their student-centered, democratic model of learning in the most improbable of circumstances.

Interviewed by *The New York Times* while she was receiving her WISE prize, Colbert reflected on how *Escuela Nueva* had begun:

> *When you see these isolated, invisible schools, why wait for big educational top-down reform from the government? We started the fire from the bottom up, by making small changes in classrooms and working with rural teachers to improve morale, results, and resources.[5]*

LEARNING IN *ESCUELA NUEVA*

Carlos has been a teacher with *Escuela Nueva* for most of his life. Like Colbert, it "has become my life project," he tells us.[6] For the last 12 years, he has taught students from six grades—early elementary to middle school—all together in one room in a remote, rural school high in the Andes mountains. When we entered Carlos's school, the president of the student council, a middle school–age boy, welcomed us. Then the secretary said a few words about the school, telling us that they were working on math and literacy in their learning guides but that they were particularly excited about their school gardens. The students were proud of their school and welcomed us with open hearts. Using grade-appropriate learning guides, they are all following the curriculum at their own pace while Carlos and the other students guide and assist them when necessary. Carlos connects the experiential learning in the garden to the math, literacy, and science lessons in the learning guides—the content varying, depending on the grade level of the particular student in the multigrade classroom. It's a highly cooperative environment—teachers support students and students of all ages assist each other.

Outside, the forest teems with life. Carlos and his students have turned this environment into a multigrade classroom as well. There is a space to watch and record observations about birds. There are gardens in raised boxes, containing carrots and other root vegetables (Figure 6.1) that, as one other visitor to *Escuela Nueva* schools has noted, "are used as staples at mealtime, often prepared according to their parents' recipes."[7] There's even a make-shift playing field behind the school, where students kick around a threadbare soccer ball during a break from classes. Nature and physical activity are integral rather than incidental to learning here. These form the content for math, science, and literacy—the subjects become authentic and real, connected to the school's backyard. Learning comes alive here.

At one point, Carlos's principal, who oversees several small schools in her cluster, rides up on a motorcycle and removes her helmet. Narda is as proud of the school as Carlos and the students. As we

Figure 6.1 Students examine plants in their outdoor garden.

walk with her, a much younger student shows us the mural at the front entrance of the school (Figure 6.2). It is a colorful map that students have made of their local area, so they and their teachers know where the school is in relation to their homes and other natural landmarks. This is the pedagogy, culture, and life of learning at *Escuela Nueva*.

The vision of learning in *Escuela Nueva* is that it is cooperative, relevant, engaging, experiential, flexible, and personalized, so

Figure 6.2 A young student looks up at the school and community mural.

children can follow the curriculum "at their own rhythm." "Relevance for us is crucial," Colbert explains.[8] "We need a relevant curriculum specifically for the rural areas." Work is often organized around interdisciplinary projects, such as the birdlife around the school that has formed the basis for learning about different animals while also providing opportunities for descriptive writing. The pedagogy and the learning are also participatory. Together, students create, care for, and observe the gardens, bird-watching observatory, and other natural exploratory centers around their school.

> Peace and citizenship are not peripheral to the basic curriculum of literacy and math, but essential outcomes in forming the character of young people who will make up the future of society.

These are not new pedagogies, Colbert insists.[9] *Escuela Nueva* was about taking good old pedagogies, renovating or recovering them, and "putting them back in Latin America" where they had a distinguished lineage—as, for instance, in the legendary work of Paulo Freire in Brazil in the 1960s.[10] The emphasis on participatory values in the schools was nothing new either, Colbert pointed out. It stretched back at least as far as American educator and philosopher John Dewey a century earlier.[11] Through school government and elections, school committees, and leadership in the classroom, this was "how you learn democracy in the classroom," Colbert explained. "Nothing that we do is new in the philosophy of education, but we do help to make it replicable"—particularly by having teachers learn the pedagogical model from other teachers and their students. In an article in *The New York Times*, David Kirp explains that "when teachers unfamiliar with this approach are assigned to these schools, it's often the students themselves who teach them how to apply the method."[12]

Personalized and cooperative learning are essential to developing these democratic competencies in *Escuela Nueva*. Peace and citizenship are an essential part of the curriculum in a culture where conflict has been rife, and a peace settlement was only finally reached between the government and Revolutionary Armed Forces of Colombia (FARC) rebels in 2017. In this Colombian setting, peace and citizenship are not peripheral to the basic curriculum of literacy and math, as they are in many other nations, but are essential outcomes in forming the character of young people who will make up the future of society. Colbert and her colleagues would likely agree with Adam Smith's claim that "sympathy is the basic emotion of democracy."[13]

The curriculum of *Escuela Nueva* is not somber, though. Children "learn through playing and interacting" in a "student-centered model." "There is a lot of talking," Colbert explains.[14] One of *Escuela Nueva*'s teachers expresses it this way:

[The children are] happy, active, engaged. We don't force them to learn things, because these children are autonomous in their decision making. They're leaders. They do things with more pleasure, more love, more happiness. They're all the time playing with and participating in their own education.[15]

In the classroom, the distinctive approach to learning in *Escuela Nueva* is supported by learning guides that are low-tech and low-cost—somewhere between a book and a worksheet—that are adjusted to each student's level. But in the end, the success of learning that is relevant, experiential, flexible, cooperative, and participatory depends a lot on the teacher. So how does *Escuela Nueva* prepare and support its teachers and spread around what they know?

TEACHERS IN *ESCUELA NUEVA*

A distinctive feature of *Escuela Nueva*, and of collaborative professionalism as a whole, is the philosophical, ethical, and practical *consistency* between the way learning is organized for students and the way learning, work, and improvement are organized for teachers. Collaborative professionalism does not compel teachers to use democratic pedagogies, as they have sometimes been required to do elsewhere in the past.[16] Nor is it collaborative professionalism if teachers are made to analyze data together to undertake swift interventions within otherwise unchanged classrooms. Collaborative professionalism is not about preparing or pressing teachers to cooperate so they can get better at a bad game where teachers collaborate but students have little or no voice at all.

Colbert and her colleagues knew that they had to educate and inspire a teaching force that was committed to the remote, rural areas of Colombia. Even more than the teachers in the NW RISE network in the United States, many of the teachers working for *Escuela Nueva* experienced extreme isolation. Many of them are the only teacher in a one-room, multigrade schoolhouse, far from peers elsewhere. *Escuela Nueva* introduced these teachers to a distinctive model of pedagogy. It also brought them a new way of thinking about teacher

> Collaborative professionalism is not about preparing or pressing teachers to cooperate so they can get better at a bad game where teachers collaborate, but students have little or no voice at all.

preparation, professional development, and collaborative support.

A distinctive feature of Colombian education is that it is decentralized. This means that teachers such as Carlos are often alone, running the multigrade schools with a principal, like Narda, who is supporting several of these rural schools in a cluster. Decentralization also challenges educators to find innovative ways (with limited availability of digital or virtual technology) to share ideas. In the face of these geographic obstacles, *Escuela Nueva* came up with three interrelated design features:

- *initial training workshops*
- *micro-centers* for pedagogical demonstrations and professional interaction
- *networking* across and beyond the micro-centers

Escuela Nueva provides initial training on the active pedagogies that are central to its student-centered model. As Colbert explained, teachers are exposed to the same methods as the students, such as cooperative, democratic, and experiential learning. The follow-up collaboration—the micro-centers—is where teachers support one another to learn, understand, and implement the model more effectively.

"The micro-center is the follow-up mechanism to the workshop for those who learn the *Escuela Nueva* model," Colbert pointed out. The micro-center model of collaboration stemmed from Colbert and her colleagues' observations of how much teachers could learn from other teachers, especially in these rural communities. "The whole process of teacher-to-teacher became so powerful for us," Colbert said. "Teachers could support and learn from one another. It was the only mechanism for them to come together and not feel so isolated."

One aspect of the micro-centers, the demonstration site, is an integral part of how teachers can learn from teachers, Carlos explained. "I am very open to receiving teachers new to the model, especially when those teachers are open to learning the *Escuela Nueva* model." By observing the model in action, teachers new to *Escuela Nueva* see the students learn collaboratively when using the learning guides. By engaging in relevant, active learning, as well as being able to put questions to the teacher hosting the demonstration, these teachers can move quickly from theory to practice to envisioning what the model might look like in their own classrooms.

Beyond the micro-centers, *Escuela Nueva* staff and supporters have also created a network, often set up around a particular cluster of schools or states. The network consists of both teachers participating in micro-centers and those who do not have the opportunity to meet regularly in those centers who continue to learn more about active pedagogies from one another. Sitting in on a network meeting in Quindío, a state in Colombia, we joined about 30 educators from all over the state who had come together, many on motorcycles from over the mountains (Figure 6.3). A labor strike for public sector employees (including teachers) was underway, but, to the surprise of Myriam, the coordinator, the teachers came anyway. Meeting in the network and micro-centers was so important to them, they said, that they were willing to meet even with the strike going on.

Carlos served as the network president in a role parallel to student presidents in the schools. He called the meeting to order. Teachers presented to the broader group how they have learned to make active pedagogies come alive in their own schools. Two of them talked about how they are using gardens as an opportunity to discuss economics, since the students and teachers are selling what they grow to nearby villages.

Later, there was time for teachers to reflect on their participation in the network and the micro-centers. Is the time well spent? What could be different? Is their participation making a difference in their understanding of the *Escuela Nueva* pedagogical model? Is it improving their teaching and the students' learning? Though the teachers are passionate about the pedagogical model, they are also aggrieved about the obstacles they face in their isolated, under-resourced, rural schools as well as government policies that assign their priorities elsewhere. The strike issues are not far away after all. The conversation speeds up and sometimes becomes heated. The teachers are as passionate about injustice as they are about their children. In the spirit of Latin American intellectual life, passion, politics, and professionalism all merge together in animated dialogue. This is their distinctive culture of collaborative professionalism.

IMPACT

Progressive, student-centered practices are sometimes criticized for being an indulgence of educational romantics that do not get results. The evidence of the *Escuela Nueva* model, however, is that it works. A World Bank study found that students learning in this student-centered, collaborative environment generally outperformed other

Figure 6.3 The network meets on a May morning. Vicky Colbert is seated on the far right.

Colombian students in more conventional public schools.[17] Another study by the United Nations Educational, Scientific and Cultural Organization (UNESCO) found that, other than Cuba, Colombia was more effective than its Latin American counterparts in serving its rural students.[18] A consistent finding across ages and schools has been the positive impact of the active pedagogies and the democratic model of learning on civic behavior[19] and on *convivencia* or peaceful coexistence.[20] After decades of conflict and violence, this is a significant achievement in its own right.

DESIGN

Escuela Nueva is the result of an intentional design consisting of two pedagogies: a pedagogy for transforming learning and teaching and a pedagogy for building collaborative professionalism and undertaking system change (Figure 6.4).[21] This design values the knowledge and capacity of teachers and students in constructing something innovative and engaging that can uplift the teaching and learning of all in the service of purposes that help transform the entire society. It provides training and learning guides as well as support to form micro-centers and networks. Teachers know that their own collaborative activity models and supports the collaboration they promote among and with their students. Teachers are not inspired and trained by *Escuela Nueva* leaders, then left alone to battle things out by themselves in their own isolated classes. There is a backbone of organization and support.

Although Colbert rightly stresses how cost-effective *Escuela Nueva* is as a model of change that gets results compared to other change strategies in developing countries,[22] it is still extremely difficult, without sufficient government funding, to network and support teachers in a consistent and sustainable way across the entire system.

When money is tight, so is time. Time pressures have been identified as a ubiquitous impediment to teacher collaboration almost everywhere, in countless studies.[23] Laura Vega, head of community connections for *Escuela Nueva,* has worked closely with the micro-centers and networks and understands the problem. She explained that "when teachers are together, when they work so far

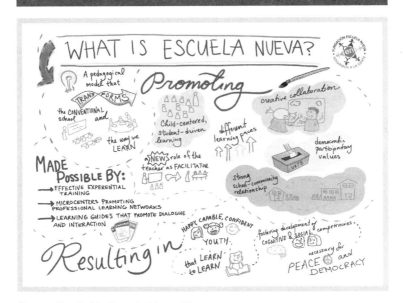

Source: Fundación Escuela Nueva Files

away, [some] principals make the most of that time [and] have them fill out paperwork [and] talk about other reforms." It is down to principal discretion to determine if collaborative time will be kept sacred or if contrived collegiality will arise as other systemic pressures and agendas take over.

Ultimately, though, as many teachers remarked, participation in micro-centers, the network, and even the active pedagogies model is largely voluntary, and when resources are short and time is scarce, other issues and demands can often feel more pressing. Vega describes how she and others at *Escuela Nueva* are helping to evolve the model to meet the challenges. "We're thinking about how we might use digital connections and technology to support teachers after the training," she says. These wouldn't replace the micro-centers, networks, or other in-person collaborations that are so important to educators such as Carlos. But they would create more opportunities for teachers to connect back to *Escuela Nueva* staff who know the model well and can provide the support, especially if a teacher either isn't participating in a meaningful micro-center or isn't in a micro-center at all.

Rural school teachers in Colombia and across the world normally do not have the time or resources to leave their one-room schools to visit other teachers' schools as demonstration sites or to inquire into their practice through micro-center and network activities. Sometimes they are able to find another educator to cover their class. But on other occasions, these teachers would have to shut down the school for the day if they wanted to learn elsewhere. This can incur a loss of learning for students. Until very recently, it also potentially exposed children to the risk of violence or other uncertainties outside of the school. Since keeping the students in school is so important, this is another reason why new elements of the model are being considered to supplement the already strong backbone.

Of course, the founders and leaders of *Escuela Nueva* can and do appeal to the moral purpose of their work. Sometimes obstacles can be overcome by inspirational leadership and by believing in the moral purpose of their teaching. Principals such as Narda, for example, see the value of *Escuela Nueva* and allow their teachers, such as Carlos, to actively participate in the micro-center so they can deepen their understanding of it and spread it to others. But not everyone is like Narda. In Carlos's words, "the goal is to make the new teachers fall in love with the model." Inspired by love and affection and a pedagogy of hope, Carlos believes that teachers will see the value of collaboration and the larger *Escuela Nueva* model and let nothing stand in their way to become better teachers for the students of rural Colombia.

The sheer will, charisma, and persistence of individuals such as Vicky Colbert, Narda, and Carlos can bring transformative pedagogical change to many of the poor in remote rural communities. But even with all of this hope and willpower, and notwithstanding a brilliant change design, the scarcity of resources and the absence of wholehearted government support can still hinder the ability of *Escuela Nueva* (and other systemic innovations like it) to be consistent across most schools and sustainable over time.[24] *Escuela Nueva* has 40 years of development behind it, a global network of support beyond it, and a Latin American culture of passion and commitment betwixt it. It also now needs a government system to stand more firmly beside it.

SUMMARY

The *Escuela Nueva* model of collaborative pedagogical transformation is, in the resource-scarce environment of rural Colombia, not a perfect one in terms of being able to consistently fulfill its purposes everywhere. Its pedagogical transformation is not always matched by the availability and strength of professional collaboration. But in circumstances of weak government funding, local poverty, and inherent isolation, *Escuela Nueva* already achieves more for its students in terms of impact than the government has achieved with students in comparable circumstances. It remains an extremely cost-efficient method of transformative change, and it persists in being a profound and persuasive alternative to top-down models of prescription and standardization that narrow what children in poverty learn to the basics and do little to improve the sustainable capacity of teachers in other developing countries. Finally, it considers how it can evolve to meet the obstacles before it head-on to ensure that teachers who want to learn about and implement the model can do so.

Escuela Nueva represents and repeats many of the features of collaborative professionalism we have uncovered in other designs (Figure 6.5).

In addition, the *Escuela Nueva* model and its widespread and long-standing implementation have drawn attention to three further aspects of deep collaboration that are also pertinent to other settings within and outside the developing world:

- *Consistency* between collaborative and critical pedagogy in the classroom on the one hand and the nature of professional

Figure 6.5 Features of deep collaborative professionalism in *Escuela Nueva*.

- Talk plus action
- Products with results
- Feedback from colleagues
- Candid dialogue
- Collaborating *with* and *among* students, not only *for* them
- Pursuing learning that has meaning and purpose
- Growing and improving sustainably

collaboration among teachers on the other—also a feature of cooperative learning for children and adults in Drammen

- *Culturally appropriate and responsive collaboration* that embraces the local learning environment as an opportunity for nature and physical activity; that recognizes and draws upon the longstanding intellectual, pedagogical, and cultural traditions that have been part of educational development in Latin America; and that assigns value to animated conversation and play among adults as well as children

- *The role of the individual as well as the group* in initiating and inspirationally sustaining a powerful movement for the transformation of learning and the teaching profession that sometimes runs counter to the orthodoxies of government policy

NOTES

1. WISE Initiative. (2017). *Vicky Colbert—Escuela Nueva.* Retrieved from https://www.wise-qatar.org/vicky-colbert

2. Hargreaves, A., Boyle, A., & Harris, A. (2014). *Uplifting leadership: How organizations, teams, and communities raise performance.* San Francisco, CA: Jossey-Bass.

3. Kamenetz, A., Drummond, S., & Yenigun, S. (2016, June 9). The one-room schoolhouse that's a model for the world. *NPR Ed: How learning*

happens. Retrieved from http://www.npr.org/sections/ed/2016/06/09/474976731/the-one-room-schoolhouse-thats-a-model-for-the-world

4. WISE Initiative. (2017). *Vicky Colbert—Escuela Nueva.* Retrieved from https://www.wise-qatar.org/vicky-colbert

5. Hamdan, S. (2013, November 10). Children thrive in rural Colombia's flexible schools. *New York Times.* Retrieved from http://www.nytimes.com/2013/11/11/world/americas/children-thrive-in-rural-colombias-flexible-schools.html?mcubz=0

6. Quotes from this point forward without unique endnotes are based on interviews and observation notes from a research visit in May 2017.

7. Kirp, D. (2015, February 28). Make school a democracy. *New York Times.* Retrieved from https://www.nytimes.com/2015/03/01/opinion/sunday/make-school-a-democracy.html?_r=1

8. The Atlantic Rim Collaboratory. (2016). *Vicky Colbert.* Retrieved from http://atrico.org/thought-leaders/vicky-colbert/

9. For a discussion of old and new pedagogies in relation to good and bad pedagogies, see Fullan, M., & Hargreaves, A. (2016). *Bringing the profession back in: Call to action.* Oxford, OH: Learning Forward. Retrieved from https://learningforward.org/docs/default-source/pdf/bringing-the-profession-back-in.pdf

10. The Atlantic Rim Collaboratory. (2016). *Vicky Colbert.* Retrieved from http://atrico.org/thought-leaders/vicky-colbert/

11. Dewey, J. (1916). *Democracy and education: An introduction to the philosophy of education.* New York, NY: Macmillan.

12. Kirp, D. (2015, February 28). Make school a democracy. *New York Times.* Retrieved from https://www.nytimes.com/2015/03/01/opinion/sunday/make-school-a-democracy.html?_r=1

13. Smith, A., & Hanley, R. (2009). *The theory of moral sentiments.* New York, NY: Penguin Books.

14. The Atlantic Rim Collaboratory. (2016). *Vicky Colbert.* Retrieved from http://atrico.org/thought-leaders/vicky-colbert/

15. WISE Initiative. (2017). *Vicky Colbert—Escuela Nueva.* Retrieved from https://www.wise-qatar.org/vicky-colbert

16. Gross, N., Giacquinta, J. B., & Bernstein, M. (1971). *Implementing organizational innovations: A sociological analysis of planned educational change.* New York, NY: Basic Books.

17. Psacharopoulos, G., Rojas, C., Velez, E., & World Bank. (1992). Achievement evaluation of Colombia's Escuela Nueva: Is multigrade the answer? Policy Research Working Papers. Retrieved from http://documents.worldbank.org/curated/en/887031468770448877/pdf/multi-page.pdf; for a summary of broader evidence, see Shirley, D.,

Fernandez, M. B., Ossa Parra, M., Berger, A., & Borba, G. (2013). The fourth way of leadership and change in Latin America: Prospects for Chile, Brazil, and Colombia. *Pensamiento Educativo, 50*(2). Retrieved from http://pensamientoeducativo.uc.cl/index.php/pel

18. Cassasus, J., Cusato, S., Froemel, J. E., Palafox, J. C., & UNESCO. (2000). First international comparative study of language, mathematics, and associated factors for students in the third and fourth grade of primary school (2nd report). *Latin American Laboratory for Assessment of Quality in Education.* Retrieved from http://unesdoc.unesco.org/images/0012/001231/123143eo.pdf

19. McEwan, P. J. (2008). Evaluating multigrade school reform in Latin America. *Comparative Education, 44*(4), 465–483.

20. Luschei, T. F. (2016). Translating *ubuntu* into Spanish: *Convivencia* as a framework for recentering education as a moral enterprise. *International Review of Education, 62*(1), 91–100.

21. Fundacíon *Escuela Nueva*. (n.d.). *Teoría del cambio [Theory of change].* Retrieved from http://escuelanueva.org/portal1/es/quienes-somos/modelo-escuela-nueva-activa/teoria-del-cambio.html

22. The Atlantic Rim Collaboratory. (2017). *Vicky Colbert.* Retrieved from http://atrico.org/thought-leaders/vicky-colbert/

23. For instance, Piercey, D. (2010). Why don't teachers collaborate? A leadership conundrum. *Phi Delta Kappan, 92*(1), 54–56.

24. See Rincón-Gallardo, S., & Elmore, R. (2012). Transforming teaching and learning through social movement in Mexican public middle schools. *Harvard Educational Review, 82*(4), 471–490.

CHAPTER
7

Professional Learning Communities

Since professional collaboration has an overall positive effect on learning, could it be introduced deliberately to bring about change that benefits students? One of the first answers in education was professional learning communities (PLCs). PLCs have moved through three generations over the past 20 years, culminating in an emerging third generation that coheres with the principles of collaborative professionalism.

THE FIRST GENERATION

Though first named by Shirley Hord in 1997, basic ideas about PLCs were already circulating under the various banners of *deliberately designed collaborative cultures*,[1] *communities of practice*,[2] *learning organizations*,[3] and *professional communities*[4] involving reflective dialogue about practice.[5] Essentially, PLCs were and are

- *communities* where educators are committed to a shared vision of student learning and development and also to each other as fellow professionals and human beings;
- *learning* communities in which students' learning improves, educators engage in their own continuous professional learning, and the organization itself learns collectively in the way it inquires into and solves problems (as opposed to rushing to judgment); and
- *professional* learning communities in which expertise is cultivated and valued, evidence is respected but not revered, and dialogue as well as feedback in the service of better professional practice is deep, direct, and demanding rather than overly polite and evasive.

THE SECOND GENERATION

In 1998, former U.S. school superintendent Rick DuFour and his coauthor, Bob Eaker, published the first of many influential works on PLCs. They rolled out their idea of PLCs globally through workshops with systems around the world over almost two decades. This body of work in theory and practice, especially in the way that many school administrators and systems interpreted it, took PLCs into a second generation.

DuFour's interpretation of PLCs[6] became the most widely known and widely experienced by schools and their leaders globally. It set out three core principles of a PLC:

1. *Focusing on specific student learning goals and interventions,* through which teachers can make immediate instructional changes

2. *Deprivatizing practice* through a culture of collaboration that makes teaching public

3. *Focusing on learning and achievement results,* using formative assessments and useful data to inform specific recommendations for improving teaching and learning

Literature reviews of PLCs in North America and the United Kingdom show overall links to positive impact on teachers and on student achievement.[7] However, the model advocated by DuFour emerged and was often implemented at a time in the United States and elsewhere when there were strong policy pressures to improve measurable student achievement very quickly in schools and across systems. This meant that PLCs often became interpreted as and equated with short-term interventions to improve student learning as represented in high-stakes standardized test scores.

This second generation of PLCs, like the second generation of *Star Trek*, was a bit darker than the first. Research by Diane Wood in one school district, for example, showed that in a context of compliance-driven high-stakes accountability and short-term tenure of the district superintendent, PLCs were overly directed from the top in ways that undermined the authority and autonomy of teachers.[8] Schools also could not allow sufficient time to develop practices of inquiry that were robust and critical.

PLCs were the strategy of professional development most favored by system leaders and professional development providers, yet teachers liked them the least of all. Second-generation PLCs might therefore have spread PLCs out across many systems, but the leaders of these PLCs often defined student achievement in terms of narrow performance goals, specified within short time frames.

FROM SECOND TO THIRD GENERATION

In many places, PLCs are now moving into a third generation. The Canadian province of Ontario represents a transformation from PLCs with the second-generation characteristics of focusing on specific short-term strategies to raise achievement results to third-generation patterns of more sustained and systemic cultures of collaborative inquiry (CI) focused on genuine and deep interest in students' learning and whole development.

This transformation has been evident over the past years in the Keewatin-Patricia school district—a district with 17 elementary schools and six high schools in the northwest of Ontario in a far-flung territory the size of France. Existentially as well as geographically, Keewatin-Patricia is about as far from the cosmopolitan provincial capital of Toronto and its vast surrounding conurbation as you can possibly get in the province. Fly in with Bearskin Airlines in January in the depth of winter and the ice cracks under your boots as the temperature plunges far below – 20 degrees Celsius. The culture and community are different from Toronto, too. Over 50% of the students come from First Nations, Metis, and Inuit populations.[9]

Ice can impede your progress when you are walking through the communities that make up this sprawling district. It can also give you a surface to play hockey on. Ice hockey, or plain hockey to North Americans, is a national pastime of Canada and Canadians. Some Canadian babies, they say, can skate before they can walk. Steve Dumonski is a teacher and a hockey coach. He is part of a students' hockey academy in the Keewatin-Patricia district that has been made famous on Canadian Broadcasting Corporation (CBC) national TV news.[10]

"When you get a kid that's on that path that you're fearful of, and you can bring him back, and he's excited about it, that's why I'm here," says Steve. Steve and his colleagues have noticed how students who experienced little or no success in the regular school environment could display surprising success, motivation, and even leadership on the ice. How could they transfer that into other environments of learning, educators wondered, including those in the regular school day?

This was no easy task. Although they have a rich ancestral culture and are often surrounded by awe-inspiring rural environments, indigenous communities in Canada, as in many other countries, have been subject to multiple historic indignities and injustices. Governments took children away from their parents and put them into residential schools that inflicted great cruelty on them, forced children to abandon their own language and culture, physically relocated communities away from their traditional hunting grounds, and, in the Arctic, even slaughtered the dogs on which communities depended for food and safety against predators.[11]

Although the Canadian government has now established a Truth and Reconciliation Commission to address this shameful side of the country's history, the legacy of whole communities experiencing multiple post-traumatic stresses has been one that includes extreme poverty, widespread unemployment, health difficulties such as hearing impairments, family breakdown, alcoholism, drug and other substance addiction, high youth suicide rates, and low educational achievement.

Some of the schools in Keewatin-Patricia have over 80%–85% indigenous students. According to provincial records, only 53% of Aboriginal students graduate in 4 years, compared to 88% of non-Aboriginal students.[12] On Ontario's standardized test, known as the EQAO, only 24% of the district's students in Grade 6 met the math standard in 2016, compared to the provincial average of 50%. Similarly, students from the district scored 56% and 54% in writing and reading, respectively, compared to the Ontario averages of 80% and 81%.[13]

When we first studied the school district in 2010 with our colleague Matt Welch, the district and its dedicated leaders (including the special education superintendent at the time, Sean Monteith) were endeavoring to engage as well as they could with the distinctive culture of their students. This included engraving into the floor of one of its schools the symbols of the seven teachings of the indigenous culture—truth, love, respect, humility, honesty, wisdom, and courage.

In addition, Sean and his district director at the time felt they had to address students' low performance and struggles with literacy and language. They and their colleagues were strongly influenced and inspired by the work of Rick DuFour in their decision to establish and implement PLCs that would promote collaborative and "open and honest" conversations among teachers about their practice, the needs of aboriginal students, and achievement data.[14] According to Sean, PLCs in the district had been around "as a vehicle for professional collaboration for teachers and school leaders for probably 15 years."[15] Led by their principals, teachers were given time to share ideas, effective lessons, and samples of work with one another to engage in tasks such as moderated marking using common rubrics in order to try to improve students' writing.

To the superintendents, one of the reasons for the PLCs was simply to raise expectations about what students could achieve. Some teachers felt that students arrived at school being what they perceived to be alingual—seemingly without language. Learning problems resulting from fetal alcohol poisoning made some students seem almost unteachable to some teachers. Teachers' deep-seated beliefs about students' capacities were disturbed, though, once they had to engage with colleagues inside and outside their classes, especially with special education resource teachers who were now assigned to work alongside them in regular classes. Teachers had strong differences of opinion about how work was to be graded, but the more demanding culture that had come into being led one teacher to say, "As professionals, we [now] feel it's OK to walk into someone else's room and tell them you goofed about something or ask for help."[16]

The PLCs began with clear administrative direction for teachers to post data walls in their schools.[17] There was also unavoidable pressure to pay attention to the EQAO test and to have children "do explicit practicing in what the test question is going to be like."[18] District administrators conveyed a strong sense of urgency to produce results and abandon previous excuses. "You can't say it's the increased number of aboriginal students coming into the classrooms," one of them said.[19] Some teachers were "terrified" of the test.[20] One district coordinator described how

> teachers are definitely feeling under more scrutiny, more pressure from senior administration. Principals regularly are in classrooms. They're doing walkthroughs. They're looking for specific things. They want to see evidence that guided reading is happening. There is a lot of pressure on teachers to make changes.[21]

Teachers were asked to reflect on and discuss EQAO scores in their PLCs. The pressure was intense. The PLCs definitely had strong second-generation characteristics. Looking back on this period, after feedback from one of our research teams, the special education superintendent acknowledged that he might have been pushing too hard sometimes because his passion for his students and their future was so great. "I realize that what I intended to be challenging conversations have sometimes been experienced as oppressive conversations," he recognized.[22]

But even as he spoke, the PLCs were already evolving from their second-generation character into being more genuinely collaborative, more ready to include a wider range of data and test scores, and more teacher led. Genuinely collaborative cultures started to evolve, and PLCs extended beyond looking at data and student work examples in teams. Teachers in PLCs were now about becoming more comfortable (though not *too* comfortable) with colleagues watching what they were doing, with building relationships, with trying out colleagues' ideas, and with believing that all students could learn and were everyone's responsibility.[23]

By the time of our visits in 2016 and 2017, Sean Monteith had become the district's director. Ontario provincial priorities as a system had evolved beyond getting students to reach proficiency in literacy and math[24] to a broader strategy expressed in Ontario's new 2014 vision: *Achieving Excellence*. This vision directly addressed issues of inequity and saw them not only as a matter of narrowing measured achievement gaps but also of paying attention to students' sense of their own identity and to special education inclusion.[25] *Achieving Excellence* also accorded high priority to improving students' well-being in their whole development as people. During this time, as Shaneé Wangia explains in her case study report on the Keewatin-Patricia district,[26] Sean Monteith had also expanded his own view of what was important for his students and their teachers, and he used this to put measured test results into perspective.

The EQAO test still exerted its influence just as it did in other boards; schools prepped children for the exam and laid out their desks in rows to simulate the testing environment. But now, as one educator indicated, "our director's pretty clear in reminding us that it's not the be-all and end-all of the world." The EQAO, she continued, "doesn't really come on the radar, other than in September when we get our scores."

PLCs in Keewatin-Patricia now concentrate on well-being and the child's whole development for its own sake and as a key to achievement. Students, the district recognizes, must first be well themselves in order to achieve well. This means engaging with the problems in the indigenous community—right down to working with families through the Aboriginal Family Support worker position they created, by giving children food to take home, and by doing their laundry for them in washing machines provided by the school. It also means building on the community's assets. In Keewatin-Patricia, focusing on the whole child is essential to restoring a whole people's dignity and identity and its opportunities for success.

A PLC for district staff—including teachers, educational assistants, school and district administrators, resource teachers, and community service providers—now meets every 6 weeks to discuss tools and strategies to help students

> Students must first be well in order to achieve well.

manage their emotions. These include creating emotion boards with faces showing different emotions, class books of emotions incorporating pictures, and modeling for students what to do when experiencing particular emotions.[27] The PLC here is delving deep, far beneath the surface of how to raise scores on the EQAO.

School-level PLCs are now run not by principals, but by teachers. Indeed, following the lead of a group of teachers at one of the schools, teacher-led PLCs have become a district requirement. The school in question is Sioux Mountain's—the hockey coach's—and the initiating PLC is one that he and his physical education colleagues created together. We came across Steve and his interdisciplinary team in May 2016, sitting around their laptops in their workroom, trying to identify the academic and nonacademic skills that students in Grades 1 to 8 were displaying on the hockey rink so that they could be made transferable into standards and rubrics for regular classroom settings. Previously, school-level PLCs in the district had, according to one teacher, been "a very top-down kind of thing as opposed to collaborative and did not support best practices."[28] This group successfully argued that teachers were now ready to run their own PLCs.

The teacher-driven PLC worked in an ingenious way. "We're linking hockey to other areas of the curriculum," Steve explained. "So, in science and math, we're able to study how the skate and stick are made, how the puck comes off the stick with such velocity," and so on.[29] "We're taking hockey, we're connecting it to the curriculum, which is engaging the students as well," he continued. Student participation in the hockey academy is also used to encourage students to attend school, decreasing absentee rates that impede student learning. In the words of the CBC television reporter, "If you don't go to school or don't do your work, you don't get on the ice."[30] Students got the point. "Now I listen, do my work. It's a privilege, not a right," said one. "Hockey academy is helping me with my confidence," another student added. "It's getting me out of trouble," an older student explained. "It is. It's helping me."[31]

The hockey-related PLC starts to convey what it is that is deep about the professional collaboration in Keewatin-Patricia and that qualifies it as collaborative professionalism:

- *It is led by teachers.* They pick the focus in a culture where they are already closely connected to students' learning and development.

- *It concentrates on the whole student* and his or her development, not only on cognitive learning or achievement scores.

- *It does not shy away from difficult professional dialogue* that poses hard questions about teachers' practice.

This doesn't mean that principals don't participate in and sometimes use their expertise to guide discussions. Also, other PLCs still address bread-and-butter issues, such as writing and math, as well as more innovative ones such as those connected to hockey.

The PLCs in the two schools we visited are also deeply concerned with student well-being, equity, and identity. After decades of indigenous culture being viewed as irrelevant or even as an interference to traditional learning—as a deficit and a source of shame—students' cultures are now increasingly incorporated into the curriculum. Teachers use examples from nature and from traditional fishing activities in their curriculum.[32] They also introduce outdoor activities, such as building fires and shelters to connect learning to students' lives in natural and even wilderness settings, where they often learn best. There are feasts and powwows; chiefs and elders are invited to be guest speakers; and Sean, the director, has been to meetings of tribal chiefs from all across the province.

These ways of attending to indigenous students' well-being are not only essential for indigenous students. They are good for all students. Elsewhere, many urban students are in educational environments that deprive these students of nature and the outdoors and thereby make their learning less effective.[33]

Sean Monteith wants PLCs to connect with the whole of who his students are. "A 'no hat' policy is not a PLC topic," he explains, half-joking. "Asking questions about our indigenous and aboriginal student population, wondering why they are engaged in some subject areas or in some schools and not in others—that is a good PLC topic." Sean understands this in a visceral way. The stigma of indigenous identity has been so great for so long in Canada that only recently has he felt able to talk publicly about the fact that his own mother is Aboriginal.

When PLCs go deeper in these ways, they do not only operate under the leadership of administrators within restricted parameters of time to devise clear strategies that promise to deliver increased achievement results. "The PLC work is dirty work," Sean explains. "Educators, teachers, and administrators like to work in a clean, tidy world. But PLCs can be messy. There may not be a finite object in the beginning or a pinpointed outcome in the end."

THE PROVINCIAL SYSTEM

How does all of this sit within the wider system? For one thing, Keewatin-Patricia's hockey program has benefitted from investment from its community partners. Groups such as Jumpstart help the school to acquire the hockey equipment. Volunteers from the local Friendship Center set up equipment and help check on students who unexpectedly leave the ice, whether for behavioral or emotional reasons, so that the teachers and coaches can focus on the students building their skills on the ice.[34] Two visitors from a nearby university approached the hockey PLC to offer internships to indigenous high school students who could assist in supporting students on and off the ice.

Second, advances in videoconferencing technology and provision of laptops with Skype facilities for students have enabled PLCs and the issues that concern them to be addressed across the vast expanse of the district and its schools in real time. Every school now has advanced videoconferencing equipment with high-resolution screens and rooms that can host over a dozen people, so educators—and also students who have to go to high school away from their families—can connect virtually in real time. The videoconferencing doesn't only allow for meetings. It changes the nature and improves the quality of professional learning. Professional learning "is not an event" anymore, one member of the district explained:

> It's more personalized. I don't have to wait for a face-to-face meeting and get all my peers together, so I have more access to expertise. I know people on the board that I can access. I think they have the ability to have those critical friends in different areas based on the learning.[35]

Third, the Ontario provincial policy system has itself moved onward from an age when PLCs often amounted to teams that analyzed student progress in literacy and math displayed on data walls in 6-week cycles based on diagnostic and standardized test assessments. Since 2014, the priorities of achieving excellence are now deeper and broader, and they are seen as part of the development of whole persons and communities, their well-being and identities. Underpinning these priorities are principles of collaborative professionalism that are supported by government and all the partners, including teacher federations and administrative organizations that work with it. A key component of this collaborative professionalism is *collaborative inquiry (CI)*.[36]

COLLABORATIVE INQUIRY IN ONTARIO

Building on the growth of CI in the province over several years, an Ontario Ministry of Education report argues,

Through CI, educators work together to improve their understanding of what learning is (or could be), generate evidence of what's working (and what's not), make decisions about next steps and take action to introduce improvements and innovations. And then they start again on emerging new issues and challenges. Notably, CI sees educators as key participants in understanding how to achieve excellence and equity in education.[37]

The Ministry lists many CI initiatives, such as PLCs, which were affecting thousands of schools in mathematics learning, middle years programs, and First Nations, Métis, and Inuit education, for example. There is no one protocol or path for CI, the authors of the document say. Indeed, they echo the conclusions of Canadian and New Zealand researchers Helen Timperley, Linda Kaser, and Judy Halbert that "inquiry is not a 'project,' an 'initiative' or an 'innovation' but a professional way of being."[38] With the aid of provincial and world-renowned thought leaders and trainers in CI (such as Jennifer Donohoo),[39] as well as Ministry and teacher federation support for the idea of teachers inquiring into and leading change together as a way to bring about continuous improvement,[40] the policy environment has enabled CI to spread throughout and become embedded in the 72 districts that make up the provincial system.[41] This environment has enabled PLCs to evolve over time from linear, data-driven processes managed by administrators to more ingrained forms of evidence-informed inquiry that have become embedded in teachers' work as a way of life.

Finally, PLCs in the district have been able to grow over time within circumstances of high stability in district leadership as the influential special education superintendent was promoted to being the district director. The district leader has been deeply connected to the school's community over a long period. He has also been open to his own learning as the district and its PLCs have evolved. This has protected the district's PLCs from the constant churn of district leadership that has afflicted similar efforts in the United States and elsewhere.[42]

SUMMARY

Since the late 1990s, among many deliberately designed processes of professional collaboration, PLCs have been probably the most widely used of all. Due to the energetic and, for many, inspirational work of DuFour and Eaker[43] in training countless school systems globally in the principles of protocols of PLCs, there are few educators in many countries who have never heard of or experienced some kind of PLC in their practice.

PLCs began as a philosophy and a set of principles, and then, in the second generation, evolved into protocols of planning and administration. This widened their reach and got many educators started with a clear framework to support them, but this was often at the expense of educational depth—especially in systems that were faced with the pressing accountability requirements of high-stakes testing. In time, though, a less-linear process of PLCs has emerged that addresses deeper and more holistic aspects of student learning and development, that uses evidence thoughtfully in combination with other kinds of expertise, and that engages teachers and their leadership as part of their everyday work rather than being driven by administrators in episodic team meetings. In short, as PLCs have acquired more depth, they have moved toward strong collaborative professionalism that supports excellence, equity, and well-being (Figure 7.1).

Figure 7.1 Movement over time of the PLCs in Keewatin-Patricia.

From focusing on narrow learning and achievement goals *to* embracing wider purposes of learning and human development

From being confined to episodic meetings in specific times and places *to* becoming embedded into teachers' and administrators' everyday work practices

From being imposed and managed by administrators and their purposes *to* being run by teachers in relation to issues identified by themselves

From serving the purposes of accountability *to* serving the needs of students

From comfortable cultures *to* constraining structures and then *to* integrated structures and cultures that promote challenging yet respectful conversations about improvement

NOTES

1. Fullan, M., & Hargreaves, A. (1992). *What's worth fighting for? Working together for your school.* Toronto, Ontario, Canada: Author; Lieberman, A. (1990). *Schools as collaborative cultures: Creating the future now.* New York, NY: Falmer Press.

2. Wenger, E. (1998). *Communities of practice: Learning, meaning, and identity.* Oxford, UK: Cambridge University Press.

3. Senge, P. (1990). *The fifth discipline: The art and science of the learning organization.* New York, NY: Currency Doubleday.

4. Talbert, J. E., & McLaughlin, M. W. (1994). Teacher professionalism in local school contexts. *American Journal of Education, 102*(2), 123–153.

5. Louis, K. S., & Kruse, S. D. (1995). *Professionalism and community: Perspectives on reforming urban schools.* Thousand Oaks, CA: Sage.

6. DuFour, R. (2004). What is a "professional learning community"? *Educational Leadership, 61*(8), 6–11.

7. Stoll, L., Bolam, R., McMahon, A., Wallace, M., & Thomas, S. (2006). Professional learning communities: A review of the literature. *Journal of Educational Change, 7*(4), 221–258; Vescio, V., Ross, D., & Adams, A. (2008). A review of research on the impact of professional learning communities on teaching practice and student learning. *Teaching and Teacher Education, 24*(1), 80–91.

8. Wood, D. (2007). Teachers' learning communities: Catalyst for change or a new infrastructure for the status quo? *Teachers College Record, 109*(3), 699–739.

9. Alphonso, C. (2017, June 23). In Northern Ontario, an Indigenous pupil finds hope for success with a coach in her corner. *Globe and Mail.* Retrieved from https://www.theglobeandmail.com/news/national/education/indigenous-education-northern-ontario-graduation-coaches/article35443965/?utm_source=twitter.com&utm_medium=Referrer:+Social+Network+/+Media&utm_campaign=Shared+Web+Article+Links; Keewatin Patricia District School Board. (2014). *About the KPDSB.* Retrieved from http://www.kpdsb.on.ca/pages/view/about-the-kpdsb; Wangia, S. (in press). Keewatin-Patricia case report. In A. Hargreaves & D. Shirley (Eds.), *Leading from the middle in a new educational age.* Toronto, Ontario, Canada: Ontario Council of Directors of Education; Welch, M. J. (2012). *Districts' experiences balancing inclusion, accountability, and change: Mixed-methods case studies of implementation in Ontario and New Hampshire* (Doctoral dissertation). Retrieved from ProQuest Dissertations Publishing (3518164).

10. Keewatin Patricia District School Board. (2016, January 22). *CBC news: The national—The KPDSB hockey solution* [Video file]. Retrieved from https://www.youtube.com/watch?v=T721qBLlA8A

11. Kirkness, V. J. (1999). Aboriginal education in Canada: A retrospective and a prospective. *Journal of American Indian Education, 39*(1), 14–30; Miller, J. R. (1996). *Shingwauk's vision: A history of Native residential schools.* Toronto, Ontario, Canada: University of Toronto Press; Schissel, B., & Wotherspoon, T. (2003). *The legacy of school for Aboriginal people: Education, oppression, and emancipation.* Don Mills, Ontario, Canada: Oxford University Press.

12. Protopapas, G. (2015, April 15). KPDSB to focus on grad rates of FNMI students. *KenoraOnline.* Retrieved from https://www.kenora online.com/local/12561-kpdsb-to-focus-on-grad-rates-of-fnmi-students; Wangia, S. (in press). Keewatin-Patricia case report. In A. Hargreaves & D. Shirley (Eds.), *Leading from the middle in a new educational age.* Toronto, Ontario, Canada: Ontario Council of Directors of Education.

13. Education Quality and Accountability Office. (2016). *School board report.* Retrieved from https://eqaoweb.eqao.com/eqaoweborgprofile/Download .aspx?rptType=PBS&_Mident=28045&YEAR=2016&assessmentType= 3&orgType=B&nF=qSFRsUhIZuVYVlyFwJBf~fslash~~plus~EV5zofI8 lnbcJhM9Lh3sA=&displayLanguage=E; Wangia, S. (in press). Keewatin-Patricia case report. In A. Hargreaves & D. Shirley (Eds.), *Leading from the middle in a new educational age.* Toronto, Ontario, Canada: Ontario Council of Directors of Education.

14. Welch, M. (2011). *Keewatin-Patricia District school board case study, internal project case report.* Chestnut Hill, MA: Boston College, p. 9.

15. Quotes from this point forward without unique endnotes are based on interviews and observation notes from a research visit in January 2017.

16. Welch, M. (2011). *Keewatin-Patricia District school board case study, internal project case report.* Chestnut Hill, MA: Boston College, p. 19.

17. Ibid., p. 9.

18. Ibid., p. 21.

19. Ibid., p. 22.

20. Ibid., p. 21.

21. Ibid., p. 28.

22. Hargreaves, A., & Fullan, M. (2012). *Professional capital: Transforming teaching in every school.* New York, NY: Teachers College Press, p. 135.

23. Welch, M. (2011). *Keewatin-Patricia District school board case study, internal project case report.* Chestnut Hill, MA: Boston College.

24. Hargreaves, A., & Shirley, D. L. (2012). *The global fourth way: The quest for educational excellence*. Thousand Oaks, CA: Corwin.

25. See also Ontario Ministry of Education. (2014). *Achieving excellence*. Retrieved from http://www.edu.gov.on.ca/eng/about/great.html

26. Wangia, S. (2017). *Internal case report of the Keewatin-Patricia school board*. Chestnut Hill, MA: Boston College.

27. Ibid.

28. Ibid.

29. Keewatin Patricia District School Board. (2016, January 6). *Hockey Canada skills academy—Sioux Mountain public school* [Video file]. Retrieved from https://www.youtube.com/watch?v=HBDC1pyve18

30. Keewatin Patricia District School Board. (2016, January 22). *CBC news: The national—The KPDSB hockey solution* [Video file]. Retrieved from https://www.youtube.com/watch?v=T721qBLlA8A

31. Ibid.

32. Wangia, S. (2017). *Internal case report of the Keewatin-Patricia school board*. Chestnut Hill, MA: Boston College.

33. Louv, R. (2008). *Last child in the woods: Saving our children from nature-deficit disorder*. New York, NY: Algonquin Books; Robinson, K., & Aronica, L. (2018). *You, your child, and school: Navigate your way to the best education*. New York, NY: Penguin; Sahlberg, P. (2017). *FinnishEd leadership: Four big inexpensive ideas to transform education*. Thousand Oaks, CA: Corwin, p. 182.

34. Keewatin Patricia District School Board. (2016, January 22). *CBC news: The national—The KPDSB hockey solution* [Video file]. Retrieved from https://www.youtube.com/watch?v=T721qBLlA8A

35. Wangia, S. (2017). *Internal case report of the Keewatin-Patricia school board*. Chestnut Hill, MA: Boston College.

36. Ontario Ministry of Education, Student Achievement Division. (2014). Collaborative inquiry in Ontario—What we have learned and where we are now. *Capacity building series*. Retrieved from http://www.edu.gov.on.ca/eng/literacynumeracy/inspire/research/CBS_CollaborativeInquiry.pdf

37. Ibid.

38. Timperley, H., Kaser, L., & Halbert, J. (2014). *A framework for transforming learning in schools: Innovation and the spiral of inquiry*. Melbourne, Australia: Centre for Strategic Education.

39. Donohoo, J. (2014). *Collaborative inquiry for educators: A facilitator's guide to school improvement*. Thousand Oaks, CA: Corwin.

40. Lieberman, A., Campbell, C., & Yashkina, A. (2016). *Teacher learning and leadership: Of, by, and for teachers*. New York, NY: Taylor & Francis.

41. Hargreaves, A., Shirley, D., Wangia, S., Bacon, C., & D'Angelo, M. (2018). *Leading from the middle*. Toronto, Ontario, Canada: Ontario Council of Directors of Education.

42. Daly, A. J., & Finnigan, K. (Eds.). (2016). *Thinking and acting systemically: Improving school districts under pressure*. Washington, DC: American Educational Research Association; Wood, D. (2007). Teachers' learning communities: Catalyst for change or a new infrastructure for the status quo? *Teachers College Record, 109*(3), 699–739.

43. DuFour, R., & Eaker, R. (1998). *Professional learning communities at work: Best practices for enhancing student achievement*. Alexandria, VA: Association for Supervision and Curriculum Development.

PART II

Deepening Collaborative Professionalism

We've heard the argument, examined the evidence, and seen five global examples of collaborative professionalism. We have begun to see glimpses of why these carefully selected examples represent not only different designs or protocols of professional collaboration, but how, in the way they have developed and come to life, they also amount to what we call *collaborative professionalism.*

Sometimes it helps to know what something is by being very clear about what it is not. Collaborative professionalism is not about being trapped in endless, interminable meetings. It is not about gathering in meetings, networks, or clusters with no clear end in view, or in pursuit of a goal or a target that belongs to someone else. Collaborative professionalism is not a device to get teachers to implement questionable government mandates. It does not devote most of the time that teachers spend together to reviewing and responding to quantitative data in short-term cycles of intervention and improvement. It does not flourish when teachers and principals are given insufficient time to develop their leadership and demonstrate their impact. Collaborative professionalism has no place for superficial discussion, fake feedback, or false praise. It should never feel torpid, turgid, or tedious, but it is not always fun either.

Collaborative professionalism does not subordinate teachers to their principals, but it does not foment insubordination against the leadership and authority of those principals either. Collaborative professionalism is not exclusionary or mean-spirited. It does not set one collaborative community against another—department against department, school against school, district against district. Collaborative professionalism does not grow in systems of envy, fear, or threat. Last, collaborative professionalism is not the enemy of positive individuality. It does not suppress the accomplishments of some for fear that this will irritate and intimidate the rest but diversifies and celebrates many individual and collective accomplishments together.

> Collaborative professionalism is not a device to get teachers to implement questionable government mandates.
>
> Collaborative professionalism has no place for superficial discussion, fake feedback, or false praise.
>
> Collaborative professionalism is not the enemy of positive individuality. It does not suppress the accomplishments of some for fear that this will irritate and intimidate the rest.

This section of the book brings together what we have learned about collaborative professionalism. First, we draw out 10 principles of collaborative professionalism and briefly reconnect these to the evidence embedded in the five cases. Second, we show how in all cases of collaborative professionalism, the protocols of particular collaborative designs are embedded in wider and longer-term cultures of teaching and change as well as in surrounding systems of stimulus (or disturbance) and support from outside any particular schools. Third, we review the key elements of progression that we might see when a school or network progresses from being a culture of professional collaboration to being a community of collaborative professionalism.

CHAPTER

8

Ten Tenets of Collaborative Professionalism

Through our review of the evidence and examples of this report, there appear to us to be 10 tenets of collaborative professionalism that set it apart from mere professional collaboration. These 10 tenets are itemized in Figure 8.1, then discussed one by one.

COLLECTIVE AUTONOMY

Collective autonomy means that educators have more independence from top-down bureaucratic authority but less independence from each other.[1] Collective autonomy values teachers' professional judgment that is informed by a range of evidence rather than marginalizing that judgment in favor of the data alone. But collective autonomy is not individual autonomy. Teachers are not individually inscrutable or infallible. The egg crate has emptied; the sanctuary

Figure 8.1 The 10 tenets of collaborative professionalism.

has gone. Instead, teachers' work is open—and open to each other—for feedback, inspiration, and assistance.

In the cases we examined, teachers were given or took authority. They were relatively autonomous from the system bureaucracies but less autonomous from each other. Colombian teachers work in a decentralized system. This inhibits access to outside support but can shield educators from constant monitoring or interference. They are accountable to each other more than they are to the system. The system still presents pressures and obstacles, but there are ways to collaborate to push back. The Ontario system encourages many kinds of collaborative inquiry (CI) as a routine part of what it means to be a teacher. Neither Norway nor Hong Kong is driven by top-down implementation. The Northwest Rural Innovation and Student Engagement (NW RISE) network teachers integrate what they are doing with system priorities, but the network is not micromanaged by any of the state systems.

COLLECTIVE EFFICACY

Self-efficacy is the expression of the belief that I can make a difference, have an impact, or achieve my goals. *Collective efficacy* is about the belief that, together, we can make a difference to the students we teach, no matter what.[2] Self-efficacy is similar to the child fending off burglars in the movie *Home Alone*. Collective efficacy is the power of crime prevention embedded in the strategy of a neighborhood watch. Indeed, that is where the idea first emerged.

Teachers and administrators in our global examples believed that together, they could do better and have a greater impact on all their students. In

> Collective efficacy is about the belief that, together, we can make a difference to the students we teach, no matter what.

Ontario, after initial misconceptions about the capabilities of indigenous students, teachers began to realize that these students indeed could learn, despite the extremely challenging circumstances that they faced in their communities. In Norway, the teachers concentrated on how to motivate their students who, the data indicated, seemed stuck in the middle levels of achievement. In Hong Kong, nobody was perfect, but everyone believed they could all improve—and this precept guided the teacher hiring process. In Colombia, educators had the magnificently improbable shared belief that they could and would help bring about peace in the future society.

COLLABORATIVE INQUIRY

In CI, teachers routinely explore problems, issues, or differences of practice together in order to improve or transform what they are doing. CI goes by many names, including *collaborative action research* or *spirals of inquiry*, to name but two. But the processes involve similar steps of identifying issues of practice, then inquiring into them in a systematic way together in order to make positive changes in practice.[3] In CI, teachers use a range of evidence to underpin the inquiry and its findings, then make plans and implement them together on the basis of what has been learned, before another cycle may begin all over again. At its best, CI isn't a separate method or process that is divorced from the rest of the work of teaching. It isn't a project that student teachers have to undergo as part of their training, suspecting that they may never have to do anything like it in their career ever again. Nor is it a funded initiative that may come to an end when the resources disappear. Rather, it is embedded in the very nature of teaching itself as an orientation or stance that all teachers possess and practice in relation to their work.[4]

Wherever they could, teachers in the case examples inquired into problems before rushing into solutions for them. In the NW RISE network, when students made inappropriate remarks online during peer feedback with students in other schools, teachers didn't discipline the students or shut down the collaboration; they explored *with* the students how to communicate online with each other appropriately by researching and learning about netiquette. The teachers in Fanling's open class inquired into the lessons they planned together, then tried to find ways to improve them. In Drammen in Norway, teachers took data seriously that pointed to aspects of underachievement that sometimes surprised them, such as the many students who did not progress much beyond proficiency. In Ontario, CI is advocated in Ministry policies, supported by influential thought leaders, and given allocated time from government funding.

COLLECTIVE RESPONSIBILITY

Collective responsibility is about people's mutual obligation to help each other. It is also about the duty to serve the customers, clients, patients, or students they have in common. Collective responsibility is about *our* students rather than *my* students. It is about our schools in our community, not my school on my own piece of land. When they practice collective responsibility, educators avoid doing harm to neighboring schools by leaving them with most of the students who have special education needs or by enticing their best teachers to transfer out to them, even in the case of schools that compete with them. More than this, teachers help each other to become better, and so do schools in the same community. Because if all schools get better, then the community becomes stronger and, eventually, the children start school better prepared and are better able to learn.[5] There will always be a need for external accountability in most public school systems. But accountability should be the tiny remainder that is left once responsibility has been subtracted.[6]

All across the world, in our case studies of collaborative professionalism, teachers took responsibility for each other's and for all of their shared students' success. In Hong Kong, the lesson and its results belonged to everybody, not only to the teacher who taught it. If the teacher in an *Escuela Nueva* school felt stuck, the students would step forward to help or the teacher could turn to other teachers in their micro-center afterward. The hockey coaches in Ontario weren't only responsible for hockey. They were responsible for all their students and for collaborating in professional learning communities (PLCs) with other teachers to help those students succeed.

> Collective responsibility is about *our* students, rather than just *my* students.

COLLECTIVE INITIATIVE

In collaborative professionalism, there are fewer initiatives, but there is more initiative. Teachers step forward, and the system encourages it or, at the very least, does not impede it. People do not feel that they have to wait to be told what to do. They understand that it is better to seek forgiveness than ask for permission. Educators are inspired and empowered to try out innovations that engage their students and reignite their own passions for teaching. And this initiative is not the product of idiosyncratic or eccentric individuals—though it may start out that way. Rather, because of expectations, processes, and funding structures in the school or the system, teachers are encouraged to share what they have started with other teachers so that they can get involved and learn from it, too.

Many teachers, and sometimes students, stepped forward to make changes in the schools and networks we observed. They didn't have to wait to be asked. In Ontario, teachers insisted on running their own PLCs. In Hong Kong, new teachers presented workshops to experienced teachers. At NW RISE convenings, teachers offered presentations on their work in school and worked with their students to share time-lapse videos of their communities with each other. In Colombia, they rode over the mountains to meet, even when strike action regulations forbade it. Collaborative professionalism is about communities of strong individuals who are committed to helping and learning from each other.

> In collaborative professionalism, there are fewer initiatives, but there is more initiative.

MUTUAL DIALOGUE

Collaborative professionalism and professional collaboration are alike in that they both involve teachers talking. What distinguishes them from one another, though, is the kind of talking. In both cases, talk is always courteous and often personal. Families are known. Birthdays are remembered. Sickness and "off days" are excused. Sometimes teachers socialize together. They also share ideas, narratives, and problems. Collaborative professionalism goes further than this, though. Talk is also the work. Difficult conversations can be had and are actively instigated where they are justified. Feedback is honest. You can tell somebody when they have goofed up. Discussion develops the back-and-forth quality of genuine dialogue, of valued differences of opinion about ideas, the merit of different curriculum materials, or the meaning of a student's challenging behavior. This dialogue isn't a free-for-all in a no-holds barred discussion. It is often facilitated and moderated, and its participants are protected by protocols that insist on clarification and listening before disagreement is expressed.[7]

In Hong Kong, teachers welcomed critique and feedback from those observing their open classes, knowing that it was shared across all of the teachers who had prepared the lesson and that it would improve the lesson itself. In Ontario, the teachers in the hockey academy PLC took skills that many might expect to be unique to the ice and shared them with science, math, and literacy teachers to make learning interdisciplinary and interesting for vulnerable, indigenous students. In the NW RISE network, teachers no longer only had their own ideas to draw from but were challenged, inspired, and pushed to work with members in their job-alike groups to improve their practice and better engage their students. One of their teachers, in fact, was glad to be challenged and no longer felt like she was the boss in her own classroom. In *Escuela Nueva*, teachers got into animated discussions about the value of their network and the constraints of government policy. Norwegian teachers were more restrained in their own ways of having dialogue, but these conversations still encompassed the big picture of the school's vision as well as technical questions about their own cooperative learning classes.

JOINT WORK

In her classic 1990 article that raises the deceptively simple idea of joint work "of a more rigorous and enduring sort,"[8] Judith Warren Little discusses joint work like this:

> I reserve the term joint work *for encounters among teachers that rest on shared responsibility for the work of teaching (interdependence), collective conceptions of autonomy, support for teachers' initiative and leadership with regard to professional practice, and group affiliations grounded in professional work.*[9]

Joint work, claims Little, is founded on a norm of collegiality that "favors the thoughtful, explicit examination of practices and their consequences."[10] Doing is related to thinking and talking in order to examine and improve professional practice.

To collaborate is indeed to labor or work together. Multiple people are involved, so this work becomes joint work. Similar to a joint in carpentry, joint work connects people and binds them together to construct something bigger than themselves. Joint work, as Little pointed out, can take many forms. But ultimately, it means making and doing something of value while also thinking about it together.

Joint work exists in team teaching, collaborative planning, collaborative action research, providing structured feedback, undertaking peer reviews, evaluating examples of student work, and so forth. Joint work involves actions and products or artifacts (such as a lesson, a curriculum, or a feedback report) and is often facilitated by structures, tools, and protocols.

In Norway, joint work was exemplified in the collective construction of the school's quality plan. In *Escuela Nueva*, joint work involved mentoring and coaching each other in the micro-centers and even in building a garden together. In the NW RISE network, the joint work was evident in the curriculum planning of the job-alike groups and in the webinars that teachers presented to each other. And in Hong Kong, at Fanling, almost everything about the open class process—the planning, revising, presentation, and feedback—was joint work in Little's most rigorous sense.

Joint work in these cases was not about rolling one's sleeves up and getting one's hands dirty, like grading a big pile of papers together or agreeing to have a colleague's most challenging student on a day when they are being badly behaved. Joint work is thoughtful work that involves dialogue as well as doing. In collaborative professionalism, talk is part of the work.

COMMON MEANING AND PURPOSE

Collaborative professionalism aspires to, articulates, and advances a common purpose that is greater than test scores or even academic achievement on its own. Collaborative professionalism addresses and engages with the goals of education that enable and encourage young people to grow and flourish as whole human beings who can live lives and find work that has meaning and purpose for themselves and for society.

In Norway, Aronsloekka's vision—to develop young people's ability and to thrive in nature and with each other—was genuinely shared, not administratively imposed. NW RISE educators wanted to increase students' engagement with their learning, lives, and communities. In Ontario, meaning and purpose were expressed in the quest for inclusion, equity, and dignity for indigenous people. In Colombia, it was nothing short of peace and democracy. In Hong Kong, by contrast, it was about the formation of character in a complex and fast-paced society. All these are much larger questions than raising achievement scores in literacy and numeracy, important as those things might be.

COLLABORATING WITH STUDENTS

In educational change, students are usually the purpose, targets, and objects of change and teachers' professional collaboration. Rarely are they also its acting subjects and participants. But in the very deepest forms of collaborative professionalism, as we discovered, students are actively engaged with their teachers in constructing change together. In this respect, student voice is the extreme end of student engagement.

Not all of the systems and schools we observed had completely moved to this position. However, the processes and practices of collaboration in both Norwegian and Hong Kong schools arose out of the principles and practices of cooperative learning and self-regulated learning that had been used in teachers' classrooms. In Colombia, students shared in the role of teacher by stepping in if the teacher's knowledge or skill was insufficient at that moment. And in the NW RISE network, the English Language Arts teachers collaborated with and through their students when they shared their argument-writing drafts across the remote divides or when they took time-lapse videos of their respective communities and shared them with each other.

BIG PICTURE THINKING FOR ALL

Education is not alone as a world where executives typically see the big picture and everyone else works away in their own little corner. In the past, big picture thinking belonged to educational leadership conferences whereas conferences for classroom teachers focused on particular skills and strategies. In collaborative professionalism, though, everyone gets the big picture.

The Ontario school that set itself up as a learning organization did so in a way that everyone did not merely see the big picture but actually experienced how everything was connected to everything else. In the micro-centers in Colombia, teachers talk about the politics of their network as well as their practical contributions to it. Teachers in Drammen create their school's vision together. And in the NW RISE network, it's the schools, not the executives at the Education Northwest Center, who determine what the strategy for sustainability will be.

Summary

If the 10 tenets were asked as 10 questions, they might run something like this:

- Are you able and willing to make significant professional judgments together?
- Do you truly believe that all your students can develop and succeed, and are you prepared to make sure that they do?
- Do you ask questions about your own and others' practice on a regular basis, with a view toward acting on the answers?
- Do you feel almost as responsible for the other children in your school or community as you do for your own, and do you take responsibility with others to help them?
- Do you seize initiative and step forward to innovate, make a change, or help a colleague in need before you are asked?
- Do you get into deep dialogue or even heated debate with colleagues about ideas, plans, politics, or the best way to help struggling children who need another way to move forward?

- Do you have other colleagues you do truly fulfilling work with—inside or outside your school—in terms of planning, teaching, reviewing, or giving feedback, for example?

- Is your teaching and your own learning imbued with meaning and a deep sense of moral purpose, and do you use your influence and authority to help young people find genuine meaning and purpose in their lives also?

- Do you collaborate *with* your students sometimes as well as *for* them?

- Do you get the big picture of your organization, understand how everything is connected to everything else, and take responsibility for your own part in all of that?

NOTES

1. See Hargreaves, A., & Fullan, M. (2012). *Professional capital: Transforming teaching in every school*. New York, NY: Teachers College Press.
2. For the origins of the idea of collective efficacy, see Bandura, A. (1986). *Social foundations of thought and action: A social cognitive theory*. Englewood Cliffs, NJ: Prentice-Hall; Bandura, A. (1997). *Self-efficacy: The exercise of control*. New York, NY: Freeman; Bandura, A. (2000). Exercise of human agency through collective efficacy. *Current Directions in Psychological Science, 9*(3), 75–78. More recently, discussions of collective efficacy are in Donohoo, J. (2016). *Collective efficacy: How educators' beliefs impact student learning*. Thousand Oaks, CA: Corwin; Hattie, J. (2009). *Visible learning: A synthesis of over 800 meta-analyses relating to achievement*. New York, NY: Routledge.
3. Carr, W., & Kemmis, S. (1986). *Becoming critical: Education, knowledge, and action research*. London, UK: Falmer Press; Hopkins, D. (1993). *A teacher's guide to classroom research* (2nd ed.). Buckingham, UK: Open University Press; Timperley, H., & Lee, A. (2008). Reframing teacher professional learning: An alternative policy approach to strengthening valued outcomes for diverse learners. *Review of Research in Education, 32*(1), 328–369.
4. Cochran-Smith, M., & Lytle, S. (2009). *Inquiry as stance: Practitioner research for the next generation*. New York, NY: Teachers College Press.
5. See the discussion of Hackney Local Authority in England that raised overall performance dramatically, in exactly this way, in Hargreaves, A., Boyle, A., & Harris, A. (2014). *Uplifting leadership: How organizations,*

teams, and communities raise performance. San Francisco, CA: Jossey-Bass. The research on the effectiveness of particular kinds of school federations has been reviewed in Chapman, C., Muijs, D., & MacAllister, J. (2011). *A study of the impact of school federation on student outcomes.* Nottingham, UK: National College for School Leadership.

6. This conceptualization of collective responsibility before external accountability was first advanced in Hargreaves, A., & Shirley, D. (2009). *The fourth way: The inspiring future for educational change.* Thousand Oaks, CA: Corwin.

7. Abrams, J. B. (2009). *Having hard conversations.* Thousand Oaks, CA: Corwin; Timperley, H. (2015). *Professional conversations and improvement-focused feedback: A review of the research literature and the impact on practice and student outcomes.* Prepared for the Australian Institute of Teaching and School Leadership, AITSL, Melbourne, Australia.

8. Little, J. W. (1990). The persistence of privacy: Autonomy and initiative in teachers' professional relations. *Teachers College Record, 91*(4), 509–536.

9. Ibid., p. 513.

10. Ibid., p. 522.

CHAPTER
9

The Four *B*s of Collaborative Professionalism

Whenever a new method, practice, or protocol surfaces in education, there is a common tendency to spread it too far and too fast, with little thought as to what else may be needed for the particular model or design to be effective in a sustainable way.

Giving feedback will fall flat in a culture of fear. Teachers will approve of professional learning communities (PLCs) less frequently than their administrators if the PLCs serve purposes that are enforced, narrow, and educationally questionable. Transformation does not transpire without trust. Reform cannot be implemented or sustained without the existence of positive professional relationships.

So, what are the four *B*s of collaborative professionalism that help us understand and also activate the contexts and cultures that precede, succeed, and surround it (Figure 9.1)?

Figure 9.1 The four *B*s of collaborative professionalism.

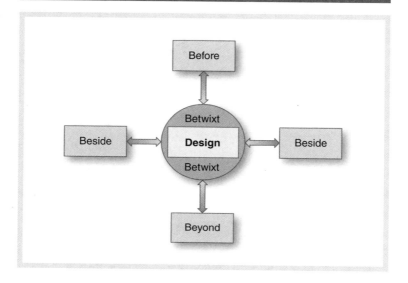

BEFORE

What came before the model of collaborative professionalism existed? Direct and short-term impact of collaborative designs will only achieve success in conjunction with longer-term processes of culture and community building. Fast change, like sprinting athletes, will not succeed unless there has been a longer and slower warm-up period beforehand. A brilliant model or system of collaboration is similar to an architectural award-winning building: It is just an empty shell unless there is a living culture that suffuses and surrounds it.

> Fast change, like sprinting athletes, will not succeed unless there has been a longer and slower warm-up period beforehand.

What goes before, betwixt, beside, as well as beyond any innovation in collaborative professionalism is almost always an inalienable part of its success. Understanding this, and having the time and skill to evolve it, is the essence and—to the outsider—also one of the greatest mysteries of inspiring leadership.

BETWIXT

What other kinds of collaboration exist betwixt or alongside the model in question in the school and in the distinctive culture of the whole society? The designs for professional collaboration that we have reviewed were not isolated, insulated instances of joint work now and again or here and there.

In all of this, the wider culture of a society is reflected in how a system or practice of collaboration unfolds in a school. The calm restraint of Norwegian educators and the love of nature they share with their children, the animated interaction and passion for teaching and politics among Colombians, and the coordinated collaboration of Hong Kong hierarchies—these are three examples of how and why systems of professional collaboration cannot be transplanted wholesale in a culture-free way if they are to transform into collaborative professionalism.

BESIDE

What support does the system provide beside the specific collaborative design in government grants, in official allocations of time for collaboration, or in wider professional networks? All schools exist in systems and must therefore find ways of being coherent with them or, if the systems are unhelpful or misguided, coherent among themselves as an alternative.[1]

The Northwest Rural Innovation and Student Engagement (NW RISE) network teachers integrated their job-alike planning with the curriculum standards of their respective states. Fanling's open class was made possible by generous innovation grants, in cycles of support, from the Education Bureau. Norwegian educators benefit from the flexibility of a broad and humanistic curriculum, rather than one that is narrowly preoccupied with literacy and numeracy to the exclusion of almost everything else. And it is supported by official allocations of time that enable professional collaboration to occur. By contrast, where a suitable system of support didn't exist, *Escuela Nueva* patiently built its own.

BEYOND

What connections does any specific design have to collaborative ideas and actions beyond the school, in overseas schools, in international research, in online interaction, or elsewhere? Internal systems can get productive stimulation from external disturbance. When new knowledge comes in and out of a system on a regular basis, this prompts the system to change and energize other systems as well.

Staying in your own class, school, or country all the time is not the way to seek inspiration. If people only look inward, they never see what's outside them—sometimes right next door. This is one way that schools fail and systems stagnate: They limit their capacity for learning.

The NW RISE schools communicate physically and virtually, despite the hundreds and thousands of miles that separate many of them. Norwegian teachers train for cooperative learning in England and visit high-performing systems in Ontario. Hong Kong educators travel to high-performing systems such as Singapore, Japan, and Shanghai, with particular ends in view of what they want to see and learn from—which has had definable effects on their own practice. The *Escuela Nueva* network now stretches across many different parts of the world, transcending the rural to inform the urban and the global.

SUMMARY

Beyond the immediate protocols of collaboration, schools that practice collaborative professionalism are global and local, natural and digital, outside-in and inside-out. They populate a *both/and* rather than *either/or* way of thinking that John Dewey would have been proud of; they are sustainable and nimble, focused on the long term and the short term, and both direct and formal—and indirect and informal—in a culture that is about action and interaction but always, relentlessly, for an unswerving greater good.

MOVING FROM PROFESSIONAL COLLABORATION TO COLLABORATIVE PROFESSIONALISM

Finally, we want to return to a framework that we introduced in one of the cases to emphasize that it applies to all of them—a framework that indicates the progression from professional collaboration to collaborative professionalism (Figure 9.2). In short, as PLCs (and the other collaborations) have acquired more depth, they have moved

Now, we can look at what practitioners, leaders, and policy makers can specifically do to make all of this happen.

Figure 9.2 Moving from professional collaboration to collaborative professionalism.

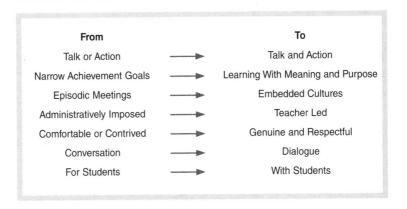

From		To
Talk or Action	→	Talk and Action
Narrow Achievement Goals	→	Learning With Meaning and Purpose
Episodic Meetings	→	Embedded Cultures
Administratively Imposed	→	Teacher Led
Comfortable or Contrived	→	Genuine and Respectful
Conversation	→	Dialogue
For Students	→	With Students

NOTE

1. Fullan, M., & Quinn, J. (2016). *Coherence: The right drivers in action for schools, districts, and systems.* Thousand Oaks, CA: Corwin; Johnson, S. M., Marietta, G., Higgins, M. C., Mapp, K. L., & Grossman, A. (2015). *Achieving coherence in district improvement: Managing the relationship between the central office and schools.* Cambridge, MA: Harvard Education Press.

PART III

Doing Collaborative Professionalism

CHAPTER
10

Doing Collaborative Professionalism

Most reports on professional collaboration and professional development typically end with a three-part advocacy for better leadership, more time, and more resources. Reports never conclude that we need poorer leadership, less time, and fewer resources! We want to add something else in this concluding chapter to the standard recommendations for time and resources, important though these are. What we focus on instead is what we should *do* to strengthen collaborative professionalism, not only how much time or money we have to do it. In particular, we ask the following questions:

- What should we *stop* doing?
- What should we *continue* doing?
- What should we *start* doing?

WHAT SHOULD WE STOP DOING?

Children, learning, and teaching must come before dashboards and digits. This doesn't mean that we should abandon data in education. Data help us track and monitor progress. They enable us to identify gaps that need narrowing and gates that are closed to some groups more than others. They can draw attention to students whose needs are too easily overlooked, regardless of intentions. These might be the quiet children in a class or the unusually large numbers of students in the middle levels of performance (as found in Drammen), for example. Data can also help us solve problems by pinpointing the reasons for issues such as low graduation rates, grade retention issues, or high teacher turnover. Progress monitoring, problem solving, and accountability all function better with data rather than without it.

But data teams shouldn't dominate what teachers do or even what they think and worry about. Too much emphasis on data analysis distracts teachers from the core of their work—teaching and learning. The alliance between social scientists, bureaucrats, and technology companies in the name of big data is overly inclined to believe it can control schools and society through pure science in a process that is linear and predictable rather than complex, improvisational, and messy—a delusion that has appealed to policy makers and academics since the 1800s.

What matters most of all is that educators inquire into what they are doing continuously and that they use the big data of numbers and the small data of professional judgments in combination as a way to inform the process.[1] This use of data should serve to improve the core of their work, which is teaching, learning, and the development of children.

Many designs for collaborative professionalism, such as lesson study, end up being ineffective when they are adopted without any consideration of the culture in which they evolved. To avoid this frequent flaw of innovation efforts, we advise that every inquiry or improvement team should have, get, or develop a resident anthropologist. Anthropologists understand culture. They understand their community's own culture—what is important, how people interact, and how the community evolved over time. They understand other cultures—the values that define them, the distinctive nature of their relationships, and how all these things have been shaped by traditions in the country and by leadership over time in the school. When an innovation or collaborative design comes to the attention of a school or a system, the person or group assigned the responsibility of acting as anthropologists can help everyone figure out what can stay the same and what needs to change about the design to adopt it successfully in one's own community.

Reform is like ripe fruit: It rarely travels well.[2] Designs for collaborative professionalism are the same. But designs coming from afar can work if people actively figure out the relationship with their own culture. Will the new way of collaborating need more or less formality or hierarchy, more or less informality and fun, and more or less prescription of stages and steps if it is to transfer successfully? Without someone playing the role of anthropologist, though, many people not only find it hard to understand other cultures, they don't even grasp the distinctiveness of their own. Cattle don't know that it's grass that they're eating. All this may sound farfetched, but some companies have been able to reinvent themselves successfully by hiring actual anthropologists to figure out their own history and story so the company can add new chapters for the future.[3]

> Reform is like ripe fruit. It rarely travels well.

Whether it is lesson study, collaborative inquiry (CI), helping another school, or being a critical friend for other educators, policymakers, principals, and all kinds of teachers must actively consider and decide how a new design for collaborative professionalism will and won't work in their own schools.

It's hard to collaborate effectively when the personnel keep changing. When leaders keep changing, schools constantly lurch from one direction to another and either teachers leave as well or they learn to wait while the tides of change wash in and out. When many or most of the teachers keep changing, things are even worse. Students start to feel that nobody cares enough to stay and when nobody else cares, neither do they. Teachers cannot collaborate with each other if they are making many new acquaintances every year. When there is a culture of high turnover, teachers behave as self-centered individuals who have to sink or swim by themselves. They feel overwhelmed and alone, and they lose hope quickly. Then they leave as well, like the others before them, perpetuating the very problem that defeated them.

High turnover can be an effect of deliberate policies that endlessly expose educators to top-down reforms and interventions. Even worse, the system or the school can be so driven by profitability that it seeks a teaching force that is young, cheap, and forever moving on in order to lower the cost of education and reduce resistance to the principal's and owner's wishes or to imposed change.

The collaborative designs that were adopted in Hong Kong, Ontario, and Drammen emerged when there had been years of leadership stability that had built a strong culture of collaboration alongside and around specific designs such as lesson study, professional learning communities, and cooperative learning. But what should schools do if this culture does not already exist, if high turnover is part of the problem the present staff have inherited?

The research of Susan Moore Johnson and her colleagues shows that teachers are more likely to stay in their school or the profession if their work occurs in cultures of collaboration.[4] Any effort to build collaboration as a leader to provide support, fulfillment, and a growing repertoire of effective strategies for young teachers will increase the likelihood that they will become more resilient and persist.[5] And, similar to Fanling school in Hong Kong, training new teachers in skills such as teamwork and appointing them on the basis of those capacities can accelerate how quickly effective cultures of collaborative professionalism can be established. The best way to develop collaborative professionalism is with collaborative professionalism. So, if you do something and get started, there is a good chance you will initiate an upward spiral.

WHAT SHOULD WE CONTINUE DOING?

Moves to establish stronger collaboration may start out simply—perhaps through having some social gatherings to build relationships or through creating teams that work on particular tasks such as curriculum development. Over time, though, the move to deeper collaborative professionalism occurs when the formal and informal, long-term and short-term aspects of collaborative activity become increasingly complex and integrated as a way of life and not only a set of activities or events.

The first challenge of building professional collaboration, therefore, might be getting some new ways of collaborating started. Once these start to succeed, though, it is important not to stop there. Keep evolving the collaboration to incorporate other aspects that help it become more sophisticated, embedded, and widespread—such as introducing more and better feedback, pushing professional conversation to a deeper level, or involving students more in collaborative activities.

Feedback is in fashion as one of the chief priorities for improvement in many countries.[6] But not any feedback will do. Feedback that is too harsh, or infrequent, or from sources lacking in credibility will have little positive impact on those who receive it. However, if we solicit constructive and critical feedback in multiple forms from a range of colleagues, not only through one isolated process or structure, the feedback will not feel awkward or artificial.

Separating criticism of the lesson, the process, or the innovation from criticism of the person behind it can be done through lesson study or robust processes of peer review. It can also be achieved by giving people roles of acting as critical friends for each other in staff development processes or teacher networks. For principals and other leaders, resistance to change can also be legitimized by asking teachers to brainstorm risks and problems associated with new programs or innovations, by presenting multiple options for staff to consider rather than forcing acceptance or rejection of one, and by dividing groups randomly into those that have the task of identifying benefits of a change and those that have to list all the problems.

If teachers are to accept engagement in feedback that has critical components, leaders must also model how they value such feedback for themselves by routinely procuring such feedback, really listening to it, then acting upon it when it is presented. You won't be successful in recommending critical feedback for other people if you are not seen as being willing to engage with it yourself.

Collaborative professionalism means not only collaborating on a bit of the big picture you have been given, such as developing a behavior management strategy or an induction program for new teachers. It means seeing how changes such as these fit into the big picture, too. Are all staff members and, indeed, students engaged in developing the vision and mission of the school? Do leaders constantly explain how specific changes or team tasks fit into this larger vision? Can teachers and students articulate that connection as well? When asked what kind of school they are involved with, will you get the same sort of answer from teachers, students, bus drivers, janitors, parents, and administrative assistants, as well as the principal?

> You won't be successful in recommending critical feedback for other people if you are not seen as being willing to engage with it yourself.

At the same time, are formal leaders witnesses to and participants in the little pictures of change? Do ministers, secretaries of education, or district superintendents get into schools on a weekly basis, hold some of their meetings there, and make announcements from there—not only in the top schools or the ones on the leading edge, but in all kinds of schools in the system? Do principals regularly go to see what is happening in students' classes, interact with students and teachers, and participate in the classes themselves—not only to monitor and evaluate, but because they really want to know? The big picture makes no sense without all the dots that make up the little pictures. Conversely, without a big picture to join up those dots, people's efforts will feel scattered and disconnected.

WHAT SHOULD WE START DOING?

If collaborative professionalism is to become more meaningful for teachers and students alike, we must find more ways to involve students in the process. Among the many global competencies that young people must develop, one is the ability to initiate and manage change—to be a successful change maker.[7] This might mean coming up with a new idea, developing a start-up company, rectifying an injustice, or building a movement for a cause. In all of these, young people will need to learn explicitly and not only by chance how to organize, advocate, listen, negotiate, inspire, collaborate, raise funds, build coalitions, and so on. Some of these competencies can and will be addressed in the formally taught curriculum. But many also arise in the hidden curriculum of how the school does its work and in what part students play in that.[8] How can students become change makers in their society if they are not encouraged to be change makers in their schools?

Students should not only be the objects or recipients of their teachers' ideas shared through collaboration, however well-intentioned those ideas might be. Students have the right to express and share their ideas as well and to have the same kinds of transformative experiences that so many teachers have enjoyed.

Of course, faced with the prospect of student collaboration in the life and destiny of the school, teachers are sometimes apprehensive about collaborative student involvement for similar reasons that administrators worry about collaborative decision making among teachers. If teachers have more collaborative rights, will teacher unions rule the roost over principals and school district superintendents? If students get more collaborative input, will they make immature decisions or irresponsible ones for communities and educators whose tenure in the school will outlast the time that many students are there? These are anxieties about loss of autonomy, power, and control that arise in all movements toward greater collaboration.

In general, people who are insecure about their own autonomy from those above are anxious about yielding it to those below. Stronger collaborative professionalism among teachers is, therefore, typically a precondition for effective collaborative engagement with students. The more confident teachers are in their own authority, the more able they will be to let go of it a little so others can have autonomy and authority as well. In the words of the Vietnamese Zen Buddhist monk, Thich Nhat Hanh, "Fear is an element that prevents us from letting go. We're fearful that if we let go, we'll have nothing else to cling to. Letting go is a practice; it's an art."[9]

Some of the cases we have highlighted show clear benefits for the value of digital technology in supporting and sustaining the development of collaborative professionalism. In the rural and remote northwest of the United States, and across the Ontario wilderness in Canada, digital and video technology is connecting teachers and students in ways that were geographically impossible or financially exorbitant a few years ago. Teachers can plan and reflect together. Students can provide peer review on assignments. School district leaders and teachers can exchange ideas and build a vision. Rural schools in Colombia are now seeing the beginning of this. In Hong Kong as in other Asian systems, enthusiastic teachers are using a range of digital platforms to keep and share photographic records of their ideas and their impact.

> Stronger collaborative professionalism among teachers is typically a precondition for effective collaborative engagement with students.

At the moment, on average, the global evidence of the Organisation for Economic Co-operation and Development is that countries that are implementing technology most rapidly are showing the least gains in student achievement.[10] But this does not repudiate the benefits of technology per se. It is more a commentary on the indecent haste and spread of implementation that is often fueled by the massive financial investments made by technology companies in climates of austerity, where other funding for public education is otherwise in short supply.

In the heated arguments for and against more technology in schools, it is time now not to see what the average outcome is but to figure out what are the best results for students with and without technology and to discern where technology can distinctively add value to collaborative professionalism that cannot be added any other way. Technology can enable students and teachers to give and receive challenging feedback that might be harder to cope with from colleagues in their own small school with whom they work every day. Technology can connect teachers who have similar interests and grade levels when those colleagues do not exist nearby, and it can give them online tools for collaborative planning and review. Technology platforms can sustain relationships and professional interactions on a month-by-month basis that have been established and consolidated face-to-face to a couple of times a year. Technology also offers ways to circulate and share great ideas and their impact in real time with other teachers, the principal, and the student's parents.

But technology is not and should not be the answer to everything. Ultimately, what matters most is that children learn well and that their teachers learn well, too. We must therefore assess carefully where investments of money and time in digital technology will add value to things that are of high educational and professional importance without significantly subtracting value from other things of equally great or even greater significance, such as physical and emotional well-being.

Organizations flourish or flounder from the head down. If teachers want students to learn cooperatively, then they should model how to work together cooperatively themselves. Principals who want teachers to collaborate with other teachers should themselves be ready and willing to collaborate with principals in other schools. What message does it send when principals and superintendents urge their teachers to collaborate, but their stance with neighboring schools or systems is to compete?

In our original design for this study, we were eager to investigate examples of systems that worked closely with other systems. One of us has previously written about local authorities or school districts in England where state schools and systems that were in a competitive relationship for student numbers helped each other, even when they struggled. The result was that all the schools in the authorities improved and more parents kept their children enrolled there. Everybody benefitted. Not only were schools strongly urged by senior leadership to collaborate, but provision of assistance to other schools was also specified in the school leaders' contracts.[11]

Wherever possible, therefore, systems should find ways to collaborate with other systems and for their schools to collaborate with each other, even when they are in a competitive relationship. We can train educational leaders in the benefits of cooperation, even with competitors. We can also consider incorporating responsibilities for collaboration and its outcomes into principals' contracts. Indeed, if your school is doing well and you want to know what to do next, one answer is to help another school.

LAST WORDS

Nothing in the world is entirely individual. Olympic medalists, Academy Award winners, and teachers of the year have undoubted talents and accomplishments, but they also benefit from years of experience, training, leadership, mentoring support, and even competition that enables them to grow over time and become the best they can be. Collaborative professionalism is about group achievements that actually enhance individual accomplishments and contributions of many kinds in countless ways.[12] Strong groups foster shared decisions, but they also underpin, inform, and enhance individual professional judgments. When law enforcement officers are confronted with a threat, when doctors have to make a life-and-death decision, or when teachers make one of the hundreds of judgments a day that characterize their classes, these autonomous judgments benefit from the weight and the strength of collaborative professionalism behind them.

In the past quarter century, teaching has made great strides in building more *professional collaboration*. It is now time for this to progress into *collaborative professionalism*, rooted in inquiry, responsive to feedback, and always up for a good argument.

Collaborative professionalism benefits the individual

and the group, it develops the student and the teacher, it expresses solidarity in the face of adversity, and it embraces collective as well as individual autonomy based on shared expertise. Collaborative professionalism welcomes rather than fears feedback, critique, and improvement. In the past quarter century, teaching has made great strides in building more professional collaboration. It is now time for this to progress into collaborative professionalism—rooted in inquiry, responsive to feedback, and always up for a good argument. Are you a collaborative professional? Are you ready for this kind of challenge? For this—collaborative professionalism—is one of the next big-step changes we can and should now make in the global movement for educational innovation and improvement.

NOTES

1. See Lindstrom, M. (2016). *Small data: The tiny clues that uncover huge trends.* New York, NY: Picador; Sahlberg, P. (2018). *FinnishED leadership: Four big, inexpensive ideas to transform education.* Thousand Oaks, CA: Corwin.

2. Hargreaves, A., & Skerrett, A. (2008). Engaging policy: Neither a borrower nor a lender be. *European Training Foundation Yearbook, 45,* 913–945.

3. One striking example is in the remaking of the fashion company Burberry. See Future of StoryTelling. (2013, September 16). *Authentic branding for a global audience: Angela Ahrendts (Future of storytelling 2013).* [Video file]. Retrieved from https://www.youtube.com/watch?v=krQG2Hceov4

4. See Johnson, S. M., Kraft, M. A., & Papay, J. P. (2012). How context matters in high-need schools: The effects of teachers' working conditions on their professional satisfaction and their students' achievement. *Teachers College Record, 114*(10), 25; Kardos, S. M., Johnson, S. M., Peske, H. G., Kauffman, D., & Liu, E. (2001). Counting on colleagues: New teachers encounter the professional cultures of their schools. *Educational Administration Quarterly, 37*(2), 250–290; Kraft, M. A., Marinell, W. H., & Shen-Wei Yee, D. (2016). School organizational contexts, teacher turnover, and student achievement: Evidence from panel data. *American Educational Research Journal, 53*(5), 1411–1499.

5. Day, C., Stobart, G., Sammons, P., Kington, A., & Gu, Q. (2007). *Teachers matter: Connecting lives, work and effectiveness.* Berkshire, UK: Open University Press.

6. Hattie, J., & Timperley, H. (2007). The power of feedback. *Review of Educational Research, 77*(1), 81–112; Robinson, V. M. J. (2012). *Student-centered leadership*. San Francisco, CA: Jossey-Bass.

7. See, for example, the global initiative on developing students as change makers advanced by Ashoka organization at https://www.changemakers.com.

8. This is argued in Westheimer, J., & Kahne, J. (2004). What kind of citizen? The politics of educating for democracy. *American Educational Research Journal, 41*(2), 237–269.

9. Hanh, T. N. (2012). *The pocket Thich Nhat Hanh* (M. McLeod, Ed.). Boulder, CO: Shambhala, p. 119.

10. Organisation for Economic Co-operation and Development. (2015). *Students, computers and learning: Making the connection*. Paris, France: Author. Available at http://dx.doi.org/10.1787/9789264239555-en

11. Hargreaves, A., & Ainscow, M. (2015). The top and bottom of leadership and change. *Phi Delta Kappan, 97*(3), 42–48; Hargreaves, A., Boyle, A., & Harris, A. (2014). *Uplifting leadership: How organizations, teams, and communities raise performance*. San Francisco, CA: Jossey-Bass.

12. The relationship between the individual and the collaborative in terms of responsibility, autonomy, and initiative is discussed in more detail in Fullan, M., & Hargreaves, A. (2016). *Bringing the profession back in: Call to action*. Oxford, OH: Learning Forward. Retrieved from https://learningforward.org/docs/default-source/pdf/bringing-the-profession-back-in.pdf

Index

in Norway, 63
second generation and
DuFour's core principles
of, 90–91
third-generation PLCs and
deepening of, 91, 95,
97, 101
Professional learning
communities (PLCs),
Keewatin-Patricia school
district, Ontario
about the district, 91–93
"big picture thinking for all"
tenet and, 118
collaborative inquiry (CI)
and, 99–100
"collaborative inquiry"
tenet and, 112
"collective autonomy"
tenet and, 110
"collective efficacy"
tenet and, 111
"collective initiative"
tenet and, 114
"collective responsibility"
tenet and, 113
"common meaning and
purpose" tenet and, 117
community partnerships,
98–99
deepening of third-
generation PLCs and,
95, 97, 101, 101 (figure)
EQAO standardized test and,
93, 94–96
hockey program,
95–96, 98–99
indigenous culture, engaging
with, 93, 97–98
"mutual dialogue" tenet
and, 115
Ontario provincial policy
priorities and, 99
overview, 17, 18 (figure)
student achievement
and, 93–94

videoconferencing
technology and, 99
whole child approach, 96, 98
Professions movement, 13
Program for International
Student Assessment (PISA)
rankings (OECD), 30, 37

Rally coach, 61
Responsibility, collective
(tenet), 6, 15, 112–113
Round robin, 61
Rural environments
in Colombia, 72, 75, 77, 83
in Norway, 59–60
in United States, 43–45, 54

Schoology, 49, 54
Science lessons, 28
Secondment (temporary
transfer), 38
Self-efficacy, 111
Self-regulated learning
(SRL), 22–25
Sharratt, Lynn, 15
Small groups and pairs, 24, 61
Smith, Adam, 76
Social media platforms, 49–50
Spirals of inquiry, 112
Spriggs, Chris, 48–50, 55
SPUR protocol, 53
Stigler, J., 30
Student achievement, 47, 93–94
Student and teacher
cooperation, consistency
between, 60–63, 77, 84–85
Student engagement,
46–48, 75–77
Students, collaborating with
(tenet), 7, 117, 135–136

Technology
data systems in Norway,
67–68
ELA student collaboration
with (NW RISE), 48–50

importance of, 136–137
videoconferencing technology
in Ontario, 99
Tenets of collaborative
professionalism
"big picture thinking for
all," 7, 118
"collaborating with students,"
7, 117, 135–136
"collaborative inquiry,"
6, 111–112
"collective autonomy,"
6, 109–111
"collective efficacy," 6, 111
"collective initiative," 7,
113–114
"collective responsibility,"
6, 112–113
"common meaning and
purpose," 7, 116–117
"joint work," 7, 115–116
"mutual dialogue," 7,
114–115
overview, 6–7, 110 (figure)
as questions, 118–119
Third International Maths
and Science Studies
(TIMMS), 30
Time pressures, 81–83
Timperley, Helen, 100

Travel, 36–37
Turnover in personnel, 131–132

United Nations Educational,
Scientific and Cultural
Organization (UNESCO), 81
University–school partnership
projects, 38, 99

Vega, Laura, 81–82
Videoconferencing
technology, 99

Waller, Willard, xiv
Wangia, Shaneé, 95
"Weak collaboration," 64
Whole child approach, 96, 98
WISE Prize for
Education, 71–72
Wood, Diane, 91
Work, joint (tenet), 7, 115–116
World Association of Lesson
Study, 30
World Bank, 80–81

Yau, Veronica, 22, 26, 27, 29,
32, 35–36
Yidan Prize, 72

Zimmerman, Barry, 23

CORWIN LEADERSHIP

Anthony Kim & Alexis Gonzales-Black
Designed to foster flexibility and continuous innovation, this resource expands cutting-edge management and organizational techniques to empower schools with the agility and responsiveness vital to their new environment.

Jonathan Eckert
Explore the collective and reflective approach to progress, process, and programs that will build conditions that lead to strong leadership and teaching, which will improve student outcomes.

PJ Caposey
Offering a fresh perspective on teacher evaluation, this book guides administrators to transform their school culture and evaluation process to improve teacher practice and, ultimately, student achievement.

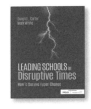

Dwight L. Carter & Mark White
Through understanding the past and envisioning the future, the authors use practical exercises and real-life examples to draw the blueprint for adapting schools to the age of hyper-change.

Raymond L. Smith & Julie R. Smith
This solid, sustainable, and laser-sharp focus on instructional leadership strategies for coaching might just be your most impactful investment toward student achievement.

Simon T. Bailey & Marceta F. Reilly
This engaging resource provides a simple, sustainable framework that will help you move your school from mediocrity to brilliance.

Debbie Silver & Dedra Stafford
Equip educators to develop resilient and mindful learners primed for academic growth and personal success.

Peter Gamwell & Jane Daly
Discover a new perspective on how to nurture creativity, innovation, leadership, and engagement.

To order your copies, visit **corwin.com/leadership**

Leadership That Makes an Impact

Steven Katz, Lisa Ain Dack, & John Malloy
Leverage the oppositional forces of top-down expectations and bottom-up experience to create an intelligent, responsive school.

Peter M. DeWitt
Centered on staff efficacy, these resources present discussion questions, vignettes, strategies, and action steps to improve school climate, leadership collaboration, and student growth.

Eric Sheninger
Harness digital resources to create a new school culture, increase communication and student engagement, facilitate real-time professional growth, and access new opportunities for your school.

Russell J. Quaglia, Kristine Fox, Deborah Young, Michael J. Corso, & Lisa L. Lande
Listen to your school's voice to see how you can increase engagement, involvement, and academic motivation.

Michael Fullan, Joanne Quinn, & Joanne McEachen
Learn the right drivers to mobilize complex, coherent, whole-system change and transform learning for all students.

CORWIN LEADERSHIP

A SAGE Publishing Company

CORWIN HAS ONE MISSION: to enhance education through intentional professional learning.

We build long-term relationships with our authors, educators, clients, and associations who partner with us to develop and continuously improve the best evidence-based practices that establish and support lifelong learning.

world innovation summit for education

مؤتمر القمة العالمي للابتكار في التعليم

an initiative of مـؤسـسـة قـطـر Qatar Foundation

The World Innovation Summit for Education was established by Qatar Foundation in 2009 under the leadership of its Chairperson, Her Highness Sheikha Moza bint Nasser. WISE is an international, multi-sectoral platform for creative, evidence-based thinking, debate, and purposeful action toward building the future of education. Through the biennial summit, collaborative research and a range of on-going programs, WISE is a global reference in new approaches to education.